# Chicken
# Wing Wisdom

©2005 Western New York Wares Inc.
All rights reserved.
Printed by Petit Printing
Layout and Design by Gracie Mae Productions

Address all inquiries to:
Western New York Wares Inc.
P.O. Box 733
Ellicott Station
Buffalo, NY 14205
e-mail: buffalobooks@att.net
Website: www.buffalobooks.com

This book was published and printed in Buffalo, NY
ISBN: 1-879201-52-6

**Visit our Internet Site at
www.buffalobooks.com**

Do you have a Chicken Wing Wisdom story in your life, or in your family's history? If so, tell us all about it and you may be part of the next Chicken Wing Wisdom book.

E-mail your story to chickenwingwisdom@hotmail.com or send it to Chicken Wing Wisdom
P.O. Box 221, Eden, New York 14057.

A portion of the author's proceeds from this book will go to benefit the Town of Hamburg Domestic Violence Office, 6100 South Park Avenue, Hamburg, N.Y. 14057. Phone: 926-0057. Website: http://www.townofhamburgny.com/domestic_violence.asp

Photos on pages: 41, 72, 84, 87, 108 and 111 were taken by Lisabeth Abt Pieters.

# Dedication

To my grandson, Bennett.

Your arrival into our family has served as the inspiration for this, my first book.

It is my greatest wish that as you grow and become a man, raising children and grandchildren of your own, that Chicken Wing Wisdom will provide you with a lasting memory of your grandmother as an accomplished woman who loved you greatly and wished to leave you a literary legacy of which you could be proud.

Love always,

Nana

# Contents

# Contents

# Acknowledgements

I've often scanned through author's acknowledgements and wondered about the people named there --- the faceless, random individuals that each author feels compelled to publicly thank. Who are these people and how could they possibly have influenced the black and white end result settled in my reader's hands?

Well, now as I dot the final "i" and cross the last "t" in my first sole literary endeavor, I have come to a great revelation about those noted in the acknowledgement section. Following months of focused research and interviews, and long nights into days of story edits and re-writes, I have learned that those who are acknowledged are the people who advise, humor, aid, correct, cajole, and, in general, put up with the writer who has dragged them all through his or her painful literary birth process.

Being an overachiever, I have a long list of individuals who have felt my writer's pain. And so in no particular order but with undying devotion and respect, here are the men, women and children who really deserve a cut of this book's profits but are instead going to have to settle for my heartfelt gratitude!

To Al Reese at the Buffalo State College Archives - for searching for images to complement my words and for feeling more disappointed than even I that none could be found. You are the true example of the wonderful people who make Western New York such a great place to live.

To Ivano Toscani, and David and Rose Mary Bellissimo - your willingness to share your treasured memories of Teressa allowed me to write about this unique lady from a fresh perspective. And the photographs from the Anchor Bar collection beautifully illustrated her Chicken Wing Wisdom story. Thank you for your time and your generosity.

To Jimmy Malczewski - for encouraging your mother to sit down and talk about her life. Her story is remarkable and one that she never would have shared as openly had it not been for your support.

To my editor, Brian Meyer - the man who helped to weave my first book into a well-crafted and readable collection. You have taken my dream of a bonafide publisher one-day printing my work and made it a reality. As rarely happens, words fail me and so I simply say, thank-you.

To my friends - who for months have never tired of Chicken Wing Wisdom occupying the center of my universe and therefore serving as our main topic of conversation. You're the best!

To my life long friend, Glenn - you knew I was a writer long before I did, and you believed in me long before anyone else. Thank you for securing my first magazine assignment and for sharing your story in a way that allowed me to craft that assignment into an excellent piece of journalism. I'm sure we'll be together again in our next life!

To Debbie - artist extraordinaire–thank you is too simple and trite a phrase to cover my gratitude for your friendship and your art. You have enriched my life and my home with your wonderful artwork that trademarks the walls surrounding me from morning to night. And now, my first book is also distinguished by the addition of your softly flowing cover artwork. You have an amazing ability to translate my words into beautiful images. I admire your ability and I enjoy your talent. But most of all I truly appreciate your friendship that never varies whenever I call for artistic help. Even a chicken wing looks more appetizing when created by your hand!

To my son James - who always insisted that I reach deep inside of myself for the absolute best I could produce (even when it meant volumes of re-writes and extra effort.) You have made me a stronger person and a better writer and I exhaustedly offer you my sincere gratitude for the many moments when my creative talents waned and you lent me yours.

To my daughter Lisabeth - from the very first column I wrote about "our friend, Erma" you have been there every step of the way with your pink pen and your unwavering support of my talent and my being. You are the most wonderful, (and most affordable) agent for which a writer could ever hope. I am exceedingly proud to call you my daughter, my friend, and a Chicken Wing Wisdom woman.

To my husband Michael - who has spent months eating cold and leftover dinners, massaging my aching writer's shoulders and taking on all of the household chores that I so completely abandoned while writing this book, - know that there is no better or more supportive partner in the world. Thank you for not making me feel guilty about letting the house go to hell and thank you for being proud of me, and my work. I love you.

And last but not least, to all the women who so graciously agreed to share their Chicken Wing Wisdom. Each of you is remarkable in what you have done with your lives and how you have made a difference in the world. I admire you all and am truly honored that through the process of writing this book, we have become friends. From the bottom of my heart, I thank-you.

# Publisher's Ponderings

*Brian Meyer*

My mom gave me my first dose of chicken wing wisdom on my fourth birthday. But I didn't recognize it as such until four decades later when I met Christina Abt.

The birthday party in our second floor flat on Elmwood Avenue is the earliest recollection of my life. I can't remember who attended, what games we played, or even what gifts I received. The only thing I can vividly recall is the birthday cake my mom made – my zoo cake.

That's because she did something special. She adorned the cake with animal crackers, giving my favorite zoo characters prime positions on this field of frosting. I was ecstatic to see elephants, lions and apes adorning the borders. When the four candles were lit, I imagined them to be fiery trees. I couldn't help but wonder if the lava wax that slowly trickled from the tops would eventually coat my menagerie.

Four decades later, memories of my zoo cake would produce an epiphany. My mom had taken a tiny action, and it made all the difference in the world to a wide-eyed four-year-old. She used a 10-cent box of animal crackers to turn an otherwise ordinary cake into a lifetime memory.

It demonstrated in a vivid way that seemingly small efforts by one person can make a huge difference to someone else.

But only after meeting Christina Abt in 2004 could I attach a name to this epiphany. It was chicken wing wisdom.

Christina, a respected freelance writer from Eden, contacted my publishing company to discuss some book ideas. One concept immediately attracted by attention. Christina talked about assembling a collection of real-life stories that would show how women's involvement with food can bring people together, forge unique bonds and create lifetime memories.

As we sat in Spot Coffee talking about whether our company would publish the book, I silently reflected on the zoo cake. And I said "yes."

The book you're holding is the product of more than 18 months of labor. Christina has skillfully woven together a quilt of diverse stories that share a common theme.

No book is a one-person effort. We thank Michele Ratzel, our long-time business manager, for helping to keep our regional publishing safari alive. Shelly, a mother of two great daughters, has imparted bucket-loads of chicken wing wisdom to her friends and family. Tom Connolly, our marketing and distribution manager, has been instrumental in helping our company to grow and distinguish itself as Western New York's premier publisher of regional books.

We also thank Rich Petit, the entire crew at Petit Printing and Scott Kropidlowski of Gracie Mae Productions for their expertise and encouragement.

My mom won't see this book. She died in 2003. It's strange, because her passing only seemed to make my memories of that special zoo cake more vivid. Indeed, small touches can make such a big difference. Thanks, mom.

Brian Meyer
May, 2005

# Introduction

I have long held a strong fascination with the wide-ranging connections between the people around me and food.

Growing up, my family never had any particular culinary traditions. Both my parents worked and neither of them really cooked. So as a result, our family meals often consisted of soup and sandwiches, scrambled eggs and toast, or warmed-up TV dinners---simple fare with no real connection to anything other than basic, life sustaining nourishment.

Yet around me I saw families with cultural food traditions such as our neighbors the Castiglias, who spent each Saturday carefully preparing and blending sauce ingredients for their ritual Sunday spaghetti dinner. I watched my friends Beverly and Jim Preston leave our neighborhood "kick the can" game every night at the same time to join their family of seven for dinner, where rotating family members created the food, set the table, said grace, and cleaned the dirty dishes. I watched my sometime babysitter Mrs. Averill patiently pass along her family tradition of special anise flavored Christmas cut-out cookies from her children to her grandchildren

In observing these and other food rituals, I began to make a connection between the act of preparing and eating food and the fellowship of family and friends. As a pre-teen I can still recall riding my bicycle to the local sub shop where, using all of my saved allowance, I purchased several ham subs. Arriving home, I opened a can of pineapple, displayed both sandwiches and fruit on colorful paper plates, and officially declared a luau for my neighborhood friends. Voila! Instant party and the memory of a lifetime.

During my teen years, my girlfriends and I would often ride an NFT bus home after school, always alighting at Kay's Drugstore where you could buy six candy bars for a quarter. Our group had a tradition of pooling our nickels and buying a combination of Twinkies and M&M candies, using the melt in your mouth chocolates as stuffing for our Twinkie treats. We would then consume our gourmet creations while standing on the corner, commiserating about the day's events or our latest love life dilemmas.

As I grew into womanhood, and gave birth to two wonderful children, I began to develop a set of food-related traditions for my own family. I borrowed heavily from my mother-in-law and her mother, both of whom were excellent cooks. Then there were also all the practiced culinary creations attached to holidays and birthdays. But I also initiated food traditions for my children that served their young needs. When they came home from school with a problem, we made chocolate chip cookies. When a special breakfast was called for, chocolate dot pancakes complete with ice cream, fudge sauce, whipped cream and a cherry always came to the rescue. In times of fever and flu, a "sickie" dinner of steak and chicken noodle soup did the trick.

The important bottom line to my food cures being the time together that they provided.

Yet at no point in my life did I so fully come to understand and appreciate the true value of food as a means of connecting people as when I went through my divorce. After 23 years of marriage, I found myself living in an apartment, on my own, with no one to cook for but myself. Not only was the experience disorienting, it was lonely.

In desperation, I invited my daughter and a few of her friends over for a home cooked meal. In addition to cooking for them and savoring their company, I intended to pick their young, progressive minds for ways to survive this painful period of my life. And so was born a tradition of women gathering in my home to share good food and problem solving conversation, which still continues today.

The women who now attend these gatherings range in age from eighteen to eighty. They are all intelligent, caring individuals, willing to share their thoughts on any and all topics. We eat, we drink, and we share our ideas. And what I have learned along the way is that women possess an innate sense of wisdom---call it intuition or ESP---that is almost always shared with food. It is a wide ranging tradition that varies only in ingredients and recipes, and one that seems to cure, or at least manage, ills of body, mind, and soul.

And so within the pages of this book, I give you the gift of 14 women who have uniquely used their own sense of wisdom to make a difference in their lives, their family's lives, in their communities, and throughout the world. I am immensely proud of these women who all hail from my hometown of Western New York. And I hope that by telling their stories, we will all come to better understand and value that special gift, which they all share, and that I have come to define as Chicken Wing Wisdom.

# Chicken Wing Wisdom I

*"She is a reluctant subject, uncertain about revealing herself to a total stranger. She agrees to interview only because her son tells her it will be good for her.*

*As I enter her pin-neat modular home, nervousness provokes her to blurt out shocking details of her death even before we are seated. Yet, clearly, the woman before me is alive and kicking, although barely able to turn her head from side to side.*

*I gently wind her back in time through her life story, and slowly she begins to relax. Three hours later, she finishes telling her most remarkable tale of taking a good idea and working at it until it's done right. At the end of our visit we two who were once strangers have become friends."*

*Get a good idea and stay with it. Do it,*
*and work at it until it's done right.*

-*Walt Disney, cartooist, television/movie luminary*

Her hands are gnarled and arthritically swollen, physical evidence of the years of hard work her body has weathered. Her head is anchored to her shoulders by an oversized rod and metal bolts, forcing her every movement to be stilted and slow. Yet her eyes---those lively and loving eyes---her eyes still reflect the vibrant heart and soul of this Western New York Woman who wisely took a good idea and worked at it until she got it right. And in so doing she changed the course of her life, her family's lives and the holiday traditions of an entire community.

Meet Dorothy Gondek Malczewski or as she is more widely known, "The Butter Lamb Lady."

While Easter butter lambs are a valued tradition throughout Western New York, they have not always been a holiday staple. According to Dorothy, only families of Polish descent featured butter lambs with their Easter meals - that is until she came along.

As Dorothy realls, "Eighty years ago my mother began making butter lambs and selling them at her market on the East Side. A company called Buffalo Butter and a merchant at the Broadway Market sold them too, but it was nothing like it is now."

While the idea of molding butter chunks into an animal form as a means of earning money seems almost ludicrous, Dorothy viewed it was a means to a very needed end. "I was married with three children and although my husband worked, he was weakened by rheumatic fever from his childhood. So I decided I should go to work to make some money. I began by working at a poultry shop in the Broadway Market."

Based on her years of retail experience in her parent's grocery store, Dorothy readily took command of the poultry shop, working 65 hours a week and attracting new customers. She recalls, "The owner would go on vacation for a month at a time and leave me in charge. While he always told me he was happy with my work, when I asked for a raise from ninety cents to one dollar an hour, he refused."

The merchant's stubborn refusal deeply agitated the young counter woman. But as providence would have it, Dorothy was soon presented with a chance to render her own form of payback.

"My girlfriend was going to buy a poultry shop in the market located just down the line from where I worked. But before she got a chance to sign the paperwork, she died. But she must have had a premonition or something because later on the owner came over to our house and said that my friend told him if anything happened to her, he had to sell the shop to me at the same price, or she would haunt him."

According to the owner, nine hundred dollars was the selling price. Dorothy accepted his offer on the spot. "I borrowed money from my mother and opened the market the first week of July, 1967. I made $110 clear profit that week and a lot of it was from people who came over to me from the market where I used to work. My old boss even came down, but he threatened that he was going to put me out of business. To which she adds with a sly grin, "By the next year, he was gone."

Although her first year in the poultry business was successful, Dorothy kept searching out and incorporating ways to improve her stand. Initially, she decided to carry pierogies in addition to her standard provisions of chicken and turkey, while a subsequent marketing inspiration evolved from a childhood memory.

"My father was an orphan brought to this country by his aunt, who lived in Buffalo. When he arrived he brought a little lamb mold, that to him was probably like a toy. His aunt saved the mold and later, when he married, she gave it to him. My mother then used the mold when they first opened their market. But eventually as she started making bigger sizes she packed it away. So when I was thinking about new things to carry at my stand, I remembered that form and asked my mother for it. She pulled it out of a box in the attic for me."

That Easter Season, Dorothy worked long nights making butter lambs and even longer days selling them. In total, she molded one hundred of the seasonal butters and successfully sold every last one.

"They sold like mad, but I got so tired," she remembers. "I used to make them in my kitchen with my girlfriend and my son. We would work until 4 o'clock in the morning and then I would shower and get to the market by 5 a.m. to set up the stand."

That sweet taste of success encouraged Dorothy to think of ways to increase her butter lamb production. She took her father's form to an engineer to see if he could create a six-lamb mold. The craftsman replied that he could easily build it, but she would never be able to use it, as her hands wouldn't have the strength to produce the pressure to form six molds at once.

"I told him that I could do anything and he should just make the mold," Dorothy boldly states. At which point, she moved on to the decorative elements of her product line.

"Butter lambs used to have a cheap paper ribbon around their necks that left a red mark on the butter," Dorothy states. I didn't like that red mark so I bought some narrow red ribbon and tried it and it worked much better. So I started cutting my own ribbon for my lambs."

Increased holiday sales led to further adjustments and improvements to her buttery product. Dorothy decided that the paper flags traditionally used on the lambs weren't good enough. So she found a man who made plastic flags with the word, "Alleluia" on them. She fastened them with red tape to toothpicks and placed them on the lamb's backs. Then she began instituting several production adjustments.

"I had more molds made, this time in different sizes and I also began making curly lambs. I set up a full display counter of the sizes, both smooth and curly. That was the year people started coming from all over and waiting outside the Market for the doors to open at 8 a.m. so that they could run right in to "the butter lamb counter."

Interestingly, it wasn't only variety that set Dorothy's product apart. Shoppers were also drawn to her butter lambs by an informational paper she distributed with each sale.

"On the paper I explained that the butter lamb tradition involves placing it on the Easter Table and during grace picking it up and announcing, 'This is a sacred butter lamb. The red ribbon signifies the blood of Christ as Jesus was nailed to the cross, the peppercorn eyes signify the light of the world, and the flag, with the word Alleluia, signifies our rejoicing over the risen Lord.' Then I added that the words, 'Peace be with you' should be said. People always tell me that they love the Easter Season because of my butter lambs and their tradition."

Dorothy's butter lamb sales increased to the point that she expanded her business to a larger vendor area located against the back wall of the Broadway Market. She also turned her retailer's eye to venues outside of the Market.

*Jimmy Malczewski at the Broadway Market stand.*

" I got this idea to go to Tops Super Market chain and see if they would carry my butter lambs," Dorothy recalls. "Their greatest concern was that I wouldn't be able to supply their demand. I told them, I promise you that I have 3 sons that will follow me. I will make all you need."

Tops agreed to order a small amount of Dorothy's butter lambs that year as a test run. Buoyed by her success, she began lobbying other supermarkets such as Loblaws, Acme, and Wegman's. To her credit, each grocery chain agreed to carry her lambs. The only problem was that the manufacturing area required for production had to expand in proportion with the increased butter lamb orders. Suddenly Dorothy's kitchen was small and useless. So with a slight hesitation, Dorothy bought an empty store near the market, hired her cousins as staff, and together they began production on a much broader scale.

When asked if she ever doubted the wisdom of her actions, Dorothy directly replies. "I did ask God for help, thinking that I was going out on a limb. But overall it worked out very well with the chains. I hired all my relatives for minimum wage and the stores were happy with our lambs. The next year they gave me bigger orders."

Dorothy's increasing prominence as the Butter Lamb Lady fostered increased year round sales at her Broadway Market Stand. By the late 1980's her hard work and determination afforded her family a comfortable life, including a large home in the suburbs complete with an in-ground pool and a cleaning lady.

Yet affluence never really mattered to Dorothy. Rather, she was driven by a strong desire to accomplish, which is what encouraged Dorothy to begin marketing her lambs across the northeastern United States. Soon she was selling butter lambs in Ohio, Pennsylvania, and Michigan. Impressively, her simple and direct business style never varied. "I would make phone calls and ask if they wanted to buy my butter lambs. Then I would start telling them what it means when you buy the lamb. That's what made the difference. Other manufacturers never understood that it was important that the lambs have significance."

With the arrival of the new millenium, Dorothy Malczewski was fully ensconced as a butter lamb baroness. She had expanded her product line to include orchid colored lambs and even briefly experimented with a butter turkey for Thanksgiving. Although, saddened by her husband's passing in 1993, Dorothy reveled in

the fact that son Jimmy had joined her at the market and, on his own, expanded their in-store product line and sales. As for the butter lamb factory, it was going strong, taking three months to produce inventory that would completely sell out in two weeks. Overall, life was good.

Then on August 10, 2003 while walking down the hallway of a Fredonia New York hotel where her son Donny had just been married, Dorothy slipped on a greasy spot in the carpet and fell in such a way that she broke her neck in three places.

"I died," she openly states in recalling the tragic event. "I remember being in a tunnel and it was scary. People would pass by and I would ask them to help me and take me back to my hotel room, but no one would stop. Finally a man who I recognized as a priest from our neighborhood stopped and asked if I would like to go out of the tunnel. He took me back and I woke up in the hospital."

Just as she envisioned, Dorothy's injuries were extremely life threatening and at one point, she did indeed die. However, friends administered CPR to revive her and Mercy Flight transported her to ECMC Hospital. Upon examination, doctors forecast that Dorothy would not live through the night. Yet following a series of surgeries, the implantation of a steel rod in her neck, a lot of physical therapy and the determination of one very headstrong woman, Dorothy has not only survived, she has returned to work at the Broadway Market on a limited basis.

"I set up my own stand at the market during the 2004 Easter Season and sold only butter lambs. It was so wonderful. People stood in line for over an hour to get waited on and they were so glad to see me. No one forgot me, and that was a good feeling."

Although she now walks with a cane, working at the market seemed to provide Dorothy with a newfound strength. "My son Jimmy told me I was crazy to try and work at the market when I can't even walk good. But the two weeks I was there I didn't use my cane, and I picked up bags and handed butter lambs over the counter. I think that's because it's what God wants me to do. To finish the butter lambs."

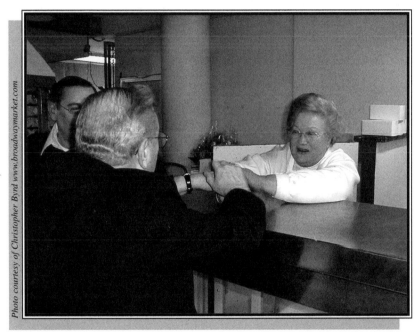

*Photo courtesy of Christopher Byrd www.broadwaymarket.com*

*Dorthy meets Buffalo Bishop Edward Kmiec at her butter lamb stand following her accident. (also in photo is Broadway Market Executive Director Richard Fronczak).*

As the official butter lamb lady, Dorothy has become somewhat of a celebrity. However there is another side to her personal for which she is equally well known in Western New York.

"I love people and I'm always giving food away. People will come and ask me for credit because they have nothing for Easter and I will just give them a ham. Jimmy used to yell at me, but I had to do it. God's been so good to me."

Today at the age of 80, one wonders if Dorothy would change her life in any way? For a moment, this wise and warm woman pauses in thought and then gently replies, "I've had a good life. Everything always worked out for me. It was hard work and sometimes I wouldn't sleep. And when I first started the business it didn't come easy with me always wondering how far I could go. But God gave me the knowledge and it always worked out fine."

She also talks about continuing her work at the market. As she and her son Jimmy have agreed, the butter lamb stand is hers to run during the Easter Season for as long as she desires. After all, as the accomplished businesswoman notes, she has a reputation to maintain.

"When I was in the hospital my doctor would come to see he and me would tell all the people in the room, 'Do you know who this is? She's the butter lamb lady.' I would be too embarrassed to say anything, but I would think to myself, 'Yes I am, and I'm proud of it.'"

# Dorothy's Duck Soup

*"Over the years people would come to the market and buy duck and they would tell me that since their parents passed away there was no one to make duck soup anymore and they wished they knew how. So I started making it and telling people the recipe. That's why I chose this recipe. It's not my favorite, but it's for the people."*

*-Dorothy Malczewski*

## INGREDIENTS

4 to 5 lb. duck cut into pieces
1 stalk celery
1 whole onion
2 whole carrots, greens and all
1 lb. pitted prunes rinsed
1/2 lb. raisins
Salt to taste
2 heap T. flour
1 jar ducks blood
2 t. sour cream
Kluski noodles, cooked and drained

## DIRECTIONS

Place cleaned and cut duck in 8 qt. pot and cover with water. Bring to boil and skim water until foam no longer appears and broth becomes clear. Add celery, onion, carrots, prunes, raisins and salt. Bring to boil, then reduce to slow boil until meat is cooked, about 2 hours. Remove from stove and take duck meat, vegetables, prunes and raisins out of broth. Discard vegetables.

In separate bowl whisk together flour, ducks blood, and sour cream. Add flour mixture to broth. Return to stove and bring to boil, stirring constantly. Once broth boils and thickens, re-add duck meat and fruit into pot. To serve place Kluski noodles in individual soup bowls and add-in broth. Note: Ducks and duck blood can be purchased at the Broadway Market and at specialty food stores.

# Chicken Wing Wisdom II

*"I've been forewarned that by choosing to interview this woman, I've committed myself to a life of service as her volunteer. That's just her way, they tell me. She lives with a goal of serving others and she involves everyone who crosses her path. So, I am somewhat surprised when we meet and I sit face-to-face with a tiny, soft-spoken woman, simply coiffed and dressed. She appears remarkably harmless. Yet by our interview's end, I am pledging my writing skills to her just cause of providing nutritional and emotional nourishment to those in need. And as I wonder at her quietly persuasive appeal, I have no doubt there is a whole lot of power packed into this tiny woman of God."*

*As we need food, so do we need emotional*
*nourishment: love, kindness, appreciation,*
*and support from others.*

-J. Donald Walters-author, lecturer, and authority
on meditation, yoga, and spiritual practice.

Sr. Mary Johnice, CSSF is an authentic Western New York,
born-and-bred native as evidenced by the fact that she has lived
46 of her 58 years within a five-block radius on Buffalo's East
Side. Sr. Johnice is also a woman who has wisely developed
ways to nourish her inner city neighbors physically, mentally,
emotionally, and spiritually through her visionary creation of
the Response to Love Community Center.

As a child, Sister was known as Marianne Rzadkiewicz,
daughter of John and Jane Rzadkiewicz. Together with her
parents, and her brother John, she grew up in a home,
prophetically located on Lord Street.

"Although I never realized it at the time, our home was like
a soup kitchen," Sr. Johnice recalls. "Mom was always cooking,
dad was always advising, and people were always coming to our
home, laying down their burdens and enjoying a meal. And now,
today, I feel as if I'm following in their footsteps."

Considering that Marianne Rzadkiewicz grew up to be Sr.
Mary Johnice, it would seem that she did indeed adopt her
parent's charitable and caring standards. Yet in reviewing Sr.
Johnice's accomplishments as Founder and Director of Response
to Love, there is no doubt that this determined woman has
created her own distinctly honorable life path.

Sr. Johnice initiated Response to Love in 1985, within St.
Aldabert's Parish located on 130 Kosciuszko Street.

Her primary goal in developing the center was to quell unrest over the closing of the parish's elementary school. Her secondary purpose involved a more personal obligation.

"My mother was deceased and my dad was ill, and St. Adalbert's was close enough to my parent's house that I could visit him every-day."

*(Sr. Johnice's Mother) Jane Rzadkiewicz holding daughter Marianne.*

Despite the fact that there was clearly a need for a community center within her East Side inner city neighborhood, Sr. Johnice recalls that she faced consistent opposition to her plan, at almost every turn, and from virtually every corner of the community.

"From the beginning, it was not easy. I had to work with determination, and often people were not supportive of what I was trying to create. The residents of the neighborhood were particularly opposed to the project because they were worried it would bring unacceptable people into their community and raise the crime rate. I was pretty much alone in my plan and there were many nights when I cried. It was a painful process, and sometimes it still is, but I always go on. If you have to depend on everyone's affirmation, you will be held back and never reach your goal."

The caring Sister's ultimate goal involved the creation of a one-of-a-kind outreach facility where people in need would not only receive food and clothing, but also learn to recover their lives. In the 20 years since its inception, the Response to Love

Center has achieved that purpose, due in great part to Sr. Johnice's unique set of organizational rules and regulations.

"We are not a soup kitchen," the petite and soft-spoken sister declares. "We're not about enabling people to just get a bag of clothes or a meal. Instead we nourish our guests with values, as well as food and clothing, and help them to recover their sense of dignity and learn self sufficiency."

With over 25,000 people served each year, Response to Love has become an integral part of the Western New York Community. Through collaboration with governments, organizations, corporations, and private benefactors, the East Side Center nourishes and supports those in need through the administration of a thrift shop, holiday meals for the needy, a Veteran's Coalition Advocacy Program, counseling and crises services, a youth awareness program, toy drives, a meal program for the housebound and elderly, and a prison ministry. It's a success story founded on Sr. Johnice's powerful "can-do" attitude, which permeates every inch of the center's building and grounds.

When people walk through the door they are politely addressed as "guests," rather than clients. Food is served in the "dining area," rather than a soup kitchen. Guests are tutored and prepared for GED exams in the adult learning center, thoughtfully titled "Sister's School." Sr. Johnice acknowledges that with every word, in every way, those involved with the center are continually encouraged to believe in themselves and their abilities.

"It would have been very easy for this place to have become a flop house, but from the beginning, people who came here for help knew that they would have to tow the mark. I'm tough and I hold them very, very accountable with a tough love."

Sr. Johnice's high expectations have produced a long list of Response to Love clients whose lives have been turned around and saved. Not surprisingly, she is able to recall most every individual who has been positively affected through her programs.

"One of our clients came to a job fair we sponsored here at the center and she learned about the AmeriCorps Vista Program. Eventually she went through the AmeriCorps training program and became one of our staff workers. Getting the job was a big turn around for her and also a great example to our other clients. And of course there are all those people who have completed their GED course here and gotten their high school equivalency diplomas. They faithfully attend classes early in the morning for 4 months and almost everyone of them ends up being employed."

Along with job fulfillment, one of Sr. Johnice's main goals at Response to Love is nourishing people's spirituality. It's a mission that she believes was given to her directly.

"My job is to bring about a change in people's lives who are broken and in need of healing. I'm like a tool or a vehicle. God does the work and I just lead them; walk with them along their spiritual journey. It's what I prayed for all of my life, not to do what I wanted to do, but to do what I was called to do."

By answering her vocational call, Sr. Johnice has unintentionally evolved into a local, regional, and nationally prominent leader. On a typical morning in her comfortably modest office, calls stream through her telephone line from area government officials, out of state organizations, and community and religious leaders, to name just a few. The conversations range from speaking requests, to lunch meetings, to consultations.

This constant clamor mirrors the equally impressive collection of newspaper and magazine articles on display in her office, all publicly praising and heralding Sr. Johnice's Response to Love achievement and success. Yet, as all who know her will attest, with each new recognition, award, and honor, Sr. Johnice's humility increases in direct proportion.

*Sr. Johnice's Father, John Rzadkiewicz*

"I don't ever want to be the center of attention for what we have accomplished here. No doubt, it's good to be rewarded, good to be affirmed, but I don't ever want to stand and receive an award for what I've done. Instead I'd rather accept on behalf of all the people, the over 120 volunteers, who stand and support me." Then closing her eyes in a meditative moment, the clear thinking nun adds, "If I start for a moment to think that I do this alone, then I will fall on my face."

While Sr. Johnice has made a difference in the lives of Western New Yorkers at Response to Love, she also has equally achieved in other places, and in other ways. Following the tragedy of September 11, she traveled to Ground Zero where she served for five days as a chaplain and counselor to rescue workers and their families. In 2002, she traveled to Washington, D.C. as an invited speaker at a national rally to save AmeriCorps. Two years ago, on her way to a radio interview, she became a local hero by pulling a child out of a burning house. In review,

Sister finds these actions fairly hard to fathom.

"Believe it or not, I am introvert and when I think about those things, I wonder, how did I do them? But then I know, I felt the lead of God and just took a leap of faith and I thank God that I responded."

*Sr. Johnice with neighborhood children Antonio Smith (l) and Robert Walker (r) at Response to the Love Center.*

Sr. Johnice pinpoints the wisdom that guides her life as, "a divine connection." Yet she acknowledges that her own spirit has also led her. "I've been called independent and radical, but I think it's more that I'm just called to do what's needed around here. I go where the doors open."

In her most recent call "to do what's needed," Sister has developed a health and wellness program for Response to Love clients. She began by single handedly raising $20,000 through public and private donations to pay for the renovation of two of the center's meeting rooms into a fully equipped kitchen and a lecture area. She then commandeered nutrition experts and medical professionals to serve as staff volunteers. She explains that the program offers a simple solution to a complex problem.

"Now we are not only giving clients bags filled with healthy foods, we're teaching them how to shop for and prepare the foods, how to eat balanced meals, how to grow nutritionally as well as spiritually."

Sr. Johnice offers that her latest Response to Love undertaking is based on a strong personal belief, one that seems taken directly from life lessons she learned in her family's East Side home.

"Before you can change a person's life you have to feed them. The mind can't work properly if the body is hungry and only when you provide proper nourishment and feed the body, can you then feed the soul. And that is a wisdom I believe with my whole heart."

As evidenced by all that she has accomplished at the Response to Love Center, Sr. Johnice is a take-charge person. She also admits to being a woman who likes to get her own way and can therefore be a challenge to those around her.

"I'm not very patient and I'm a perfectionist who likes things to be done the right way. But I am learning to let things happen in God's way in God's time. So many times I have prayed with clenched fists instead of open hands, and so I am trying to learn to open my hands and ask God to fill them with what he wants me to do."

When asked if she believes her new found wisdom is working, the good Sister sweetly smiles and replies, "Well, it's not easy, but then again, I'm finding that with my hands open, miracles do happen everyday."

# Sr. Mary Johnice's Cheese Souffle

*"I love to cook. This was one of the first souffles I ever made and it turned out perfectly. It's not time consuming and it's really delicious. It's a simple kind of meal along the style served at the Benedictine Monastery."*

-*Sr. Mary Johnice*

## INGREDIENTS

10 to 12 slices of white bread (crusts removed)
1 lb. Sharp cheddar cheese, grated
3 eggs
2 cu. Milk
1 medium onion, chopped
2 t Nance's sharp and creamy mustard

## DIRECTIONS

• Cut bread into small cubes.

• Sprinkle grated cheese over bread and mix.

• In a small bowl beat eggs, milk and mustard.

• Mix in chopped onion.

• Pour mixture over the bread and cheese.

• Pour all ingredients into a greased 1 quart casserole dish.

• Refrigerate overnight.

• Cut crusts from bread into small cubes and fry in 1/2 cup margarine.

• Sprinkle on top of casserole before baking.

• Bake at 325 degrees for 45-55 minutes until knife inserted in center of casserole comes out clean.

# Chicken Wing Wisdom III

*"As she multi-tasks arranging flowers, answering phone calls, wiping glasses, and checking the daily specials, she exudes a clear-cut confidence. The third generation of her family to stand behind the dark mahogany bar, this woman definitely knows who she is, by virtue of where she came from. After taking over the business from her father and her father's father, she instinctively welcomes diners as family, easily suggesting food choices that she knows will delight. It's all just as she imagined, despite the many changes she endured along the way."*

*Life is about not knowing, having to change,
taking the moment and making the best of it without
knowing what's going to happen next.*

*-Gilda Radner*

The year was 1981. Bethlehem Steel was on the verge of closing its principal Lackawanna mills, with other related Western New York industries soon to follow. It was a time of disorientation and devastation for the Queen City on the Lake.

Yet the men who gave muscle and might to those Lackawanna mills were equally tough in their minds and spirits. They were union workers united in both resolve and belief that no matter how dire the circumstances, they would always survive.

The year was 1981. Twenty-year old Krista Van Wagner was newly graduated from the prestigious Culinary Institute of America (CIA). Upon earning her degree in culinary arts, Krista decided to return to her family's homestead, the center of which was their landmark Lackawanna bar, Curly's. It was a time of excitement and expectation for this young woman with an epicurean dream.

Like most of her family, Krista worked at Curly's from an early age. So, it was easy for the new graduate to once again slip behind the saloon's dark wooden bar and tend to the union workers who long considered Curly's their second home.

As Krista poured beers and shots for the regulars, she shared details of her CIA experience. She told of a restaurant design course in which she used Curly's as her subject. She eagerly described renovations and new menu options, which she envisioned actually incorporating into the family's bar/restaurant.

"I was so excited about my plan," Krista recalls. "I was going to take out the pool tables in the back room and replace them with tables and chairs where people could sit and enjoy meals, and I created a really wonderful menu. But as soon as I began talking about it, the steelworkers told me that I dare not even think about coming back and changing my father's gold mine. They said that the unions would never die --- that they would always be around --- and since Curly's was just the way they liked it, I needed to leave it alone."

*1955 photo of Curly's Bar, and steel worker patrons. Pictured left to right Joe McMurray, Jim O'Hara, Tommy Walton, Jake Winslow, Eddie Fields and Paul Warthling (Krista's father) tending bar.*

Responding to their adverse reactions Krista took the moment and made the best of it, completely changing her career plans without any idea of what might follow. As it turned out, Krista's choices ended up taking her halfway around the world and home again. All the way home to Curly's.

Krista's revamped career plan began with a brief kitchen stint at Daffodil's Restaurant in Williamsville. It wasn't long however before she exchanged her close-to-home employment for a globe trotting, chef-in-training adventure that began at Harrah's Hotel in Lake Tahoe, and continued on to The Ambiance Jamaica Resort in Jamaica, The Grand Pavilion Hotel in Grand Cayman, The Gstaad Palace Hotel in Paris, and The Park Plaza Gardens Hotel in Florida. While each locale offered essential and indigenous culinary experiences, Krista notes that there was one continual obstacle.

"It was tough for me working in the restaurant industry. The staff at many of the places where I worked was mostly men, and they always picked on me. But I love the challenge of learning something new and I believed I could do the work. So despite the fact that I thought being a woman in the restaurant business would kill me, it actually made me successful."

The feisty chef's level of professional accomplishment truly began to soar in 1990 when she returned home to Curly's, this time accompanied by her husband/chef, Chef Kirk Van Wagner.

"Kirk and I had been friends since culinary school and we both worked in Florida at the same time," Krista recalls. "On the night before I was leaving Florida for Jamaica, Kirk and I were out celebrating and we danced. That was it. We fell in love with that one dance."

When Krista and Kirk made the return trek to Lackawanna they did so out of familial devotion. Krista's father was temporarily unable to work due to a broken foot. His injury coupled with the drop in bar trade following the steel mill closings,was seriously threatening Curly's bottom line. So the chef duo agreed to move back and reorganize the family owned business. This time when

Krista pronounced renovation and revision plans, not a protest was heard.

"At that point, the kitchen was closed and the bar was the only thing running," Krista remembers. "So we closed down for a couple of weeks and scrubbed the floors and cleaned the place out." With a devilish grin she adds, "I got rid of all the pool tables in the back too."

In September of 1990 Curly's reopened with the same revered name and storefront, but with a freshly updated interior and a dramatically different menu. Not surprisingly, customer acceptance was slow in coming. In fact, many neighborhood patrons and bar regulars walked in, turned around and walked out. Yet those who remained were treated to a high level of culinary excellence within the welcoming family ambience that had long defined the Lackawanna landmark.

In their early days, Kirk and Krista ran the restaurant with a very limited staff. Together the two handled all the kitchen and cleaning chores while Krista additionally hustled in the dining room, taking orders and serving food. As business improved, Krista's younger brother helped as a willing but completely inexperienced waiter. It was a situation that still provides Krista with one of her favorite Curly's stories.

"The dining room began filling up one night and I knew I couldn't handle it alone. So I called in my younger brother who had never worked in a restaurant before. At one point I sent him over to offer dessert to a table, forgetting that he didn't even know the dessert menu. Later the woman at that table called me over to thank me for her dinner. She also informed me that she was Janice Okun, restaurant critic for The Buffalo News and while she rarely spoke directly to restaurant owners, she advised me to call in a few more friends to help out because she was going to review Curly's and once it appeared in the paper, we were going to need the help."

As Okun predicted, her three-star review immediately encouraged discriminating diners from across Western New York and Southern Canada to find their way to the unassuming eatery. While the positive critique provided much needed exposure, the quality and flavor of Curly's food kept customers coming back as they became willing partners in Krista's Jamaican food love affair.

*Krista with her parents, Marian and Paul Warthling.*

"I fell in love with the spices and flavors of Jamaica when I first moved there in 1985. Then later I moved to Grand Cayman and lived in a town that was actually named 'Hell'. While I was waiting for my work permits there, I spent my free time developing a hot sauce that I named, Hell Sauce. I bottled it and sold it in a souvenir shop down

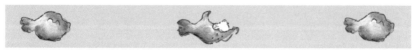

there. My inspiration for it came from the fact that I could never get chicken wings hot enough for the men at Curly's bar. So I wanted to make a sauce that I could go back home and really make them hot. That sauce definitely got them!"

In addition to spicy fare, Krista also developed her own Jamaican Jerk Sauce and Marinade, a sweet and tangy Caribbean version of a barbecue sauce. Soon "Jerk" became the signature item on Curly's menu as Krista and Kirk paired it with every-thing from chicken wings to pork loins.

Within two years of opening, Krista and Kirk creatively transformed Curly's into a Western New York restaurant of popular choice. As a means of further advancing their success, Krista began cooking on local television shows, running cooking classes at local supermarkets and participating in a number of food-related community fund raisers.

Curly's also began earning culinary acclaim at area events such as the Taste of Buffalo where they were chosen as Best Food/Jamaican Jerk Chicken in 1991, People's Choice Award/Jamaican Jerk Chicken in 1992 and Best Dessert/Mile High Peanut Butter Pie in 1993. Krista's energetic personality made her a public relations natural. Her savory sauces and skillfully prepared foods placed her in great demand. The blending of both made the names Krista and Curly's synonymous throughout Western New York.

While Krista was building her culinary renown, she was also shaping her personal life as the mother of three. Son Erik and daughters Lianne and Maggie were born in 1993, 1995, and 1996, respectively. However their arrivals did little to slow the dynamic chef's professional pace.

In addition to managing Curly's promotional work and sharing restaurant responsibilities, Krista began assuming a significant amount of volunteer committee work with organizations such as The United Way, the Erie County Youth Board, the Lackawanna Youth Board and the Lackawanna Community Building Team. She also started teaching a Restaurant and Hospitality Management Course at Trocaire College.

Then one night while working the dining room, Krista's life took an abrupt turn.

"This customer sat down at the bar and started talking to me," Krista recalls. "We talked about life and I told her all the things I was doing and how busy I was. She looked at me and told me that I was missing out on the important things in life, especially my children. I thought about it and realized she was right. So, two years ago, I scaled everything back so I could spend more time with them."

Krista's definition of scaling back meant giving up her kitchen responsibilities at Curly's and withdrawing from teaching and most of her volunteer work. Yet she continued to maintain the restaurant's books, arrange all the catering jobs, teach a full range of cooking classes and take on occasional Saturday night hostess assignments.

In reviewing a schedule that many would assess as full, Krista instead notes a void.

"I love what I'm doing now. I love my kids and I am so glad that I am home with them after school. They get me involved in their school projects and I do cooking demonstrations for their classes; they keep me busy all the time. But just the other day, I threw my chef's coat on, for no special reason, and I realized that I really miss cooking at the restaurant."

Her regrets quickly vanish however as Krista turns her focus to the sole community outreach project she has continued to foster.

*Photo Courtesy of Cheryl Gorski Photography (cherylgorski.com)*

*Krista Van Wagner*

"For the last 7 years I have worked with a local group of dentists and volunteers led by Dr. Bill Mahre. Each spring we travel to the Dominican Republic and provide free dental work for people there in need."

As she explains the volunteer project, Krista's entire body energizes.

"I love the work. We set up our clinic in a field in the mountains and end up seeing about 100 people each day. On one trip alone we performed $100,000 worth of restorative dental work during the three days we were there."

When asked about the challenge of undertaking a project in which she has no formal training, Krista responds in her typical life-embracing form.

"The instruments that the dentists use look like cooking tools to me. Besides, where else could you get an experience like that?"

The stark realities of her dental clinic experiences have encouraged Krista to return to Curly's kitchen. As a means of raising money for needy children in the Dominican Republic, the good-hearted chef has created a recipe for Dominican Gold Chocolate Chip Cookies, now available on both Curly's restaurant and catering menus.

The gold in the title refers to a special type of vanilla, available only in the Dominican Republic. Krista discovered the savory flavor on one of her good will journeys. "It has a strong taste of cinnamon that gives it such a great flavor. We serve the cookies warm in the restaurant and they smell so good. People really love them."

Whether creating fund raising cookie recipes or whipping up favorite meals for her family, there is no doubt that Krista Van Wagner was born to cook. It is clearly her gift and her passion. It is also why, despite her best-intentioned commitment to spend more time with her children, she recently put the finishing touches on an expansive food-related business deal.

"I just signed the paperwork to buy the building next door to Curly's where I'm going to run our banquet facility, and I'm also going to set up my cooking school. It's always been my dream to run a cooking school and now I can actually see it. I know I'm going to get my dream."

Krista's plans call for Curly's annex to be up and running by early 2006. She and Kirk will jointly undertake the new venture by interconnecting the kitchens of both facilities. As for the restaurant side of Curly's, Krista notes that it will be business as usual with their long running and loyal staff of 31 employees taking care of customers, her dad running the bar, and her mom occasionally supervising the dining room.

"Curly's has always been run by our family starting with my grandparents Curly and Mae through my parents and now Kirk and I. So I know it will be fine."

There is no doubt that family provides the foundation for Krista Inez Warthling Van Wagners's life. In reviewing her many professional successes, she credits her parents and her husband for their individual wisdoms as well as their constant love and support. She acknowledges the influence of significant friends such as Sister Agnetta, a home economics teacher at her high school alma mater, Immaculata Academy, who introduced Krista to the CIA. She also credits Laura Mulqueen, a long time Curly's employee who first started Krista in the kitchen at the tender age of 12 and worked with her there for years.

Yet whether talking about family, friends or Curly's customers, Krista pointedly preaches a wisdom that reverts to her passion for creating and sharing food.

"If I could, I would have only round tables -- at Curly's, in my home, everywhere that people eat together. For when you bring people together at a round table,-- the food, the conversation, the love -- everything flows around the table with no end."

# Krista's Escovitche

*"I first tasted this recipe when I lived in Jamaica and I fell in love with it because of its purpose. Jamaican fisherman would make it for lunch every day using whatever fresh fish they caught. The original recipe used a pickled base and was very heavy with vinegar and so I modified it to make it lighter. I did however continue to use ketchup to bind the ingredients just as they do in Jamiaca. People make fun of me using ketchup but it really gives the dish a great taste."*

*-Krista VanWagner*

## INGREDIENTS

2-8oz. Portions red snapper filet

1 T lemon juice

salt and pepper

flour

## SAUCE

Julienne of red, green, and yellow peppers, onion and tomatoes.

2 oz. butter

1 clove garlic, sliced

2 sprigs fresh thyme

4 oz. white wine

2 oz. white vinegar

4 oz. ketchup

Hot sauce to taste

Worcestershire sauce to taste.

## DIRECTIONS

Season snapper filet with salt, pepper and lemon juice. Dredge in flour. Brown both sides of snapper in hot oil. Discard excess oil. With fish still in pan, add in butter, peppers, thyme, onion and tomatoes and sauté. Deglaze with wine and vinegar. Add ketchup. Season with hot sauce and Worcestershire Sauce.

# Chicken Wing Wisdom IV

*"Sitting across from her, I am comfortably enveloped
by her warm personality and entranced by her
deep-blue eyes.  It's hard to imagine that this
woman of all around beauty ever suffered from a
life-threatening illness of her own making.
She is soft spoken, quick to laugh, thoughtful,
and yet somehow always guarded, always testing
for possible invaders into her now safe and balanced
world. Safety is the key word in this woman's life.
Safety for herself, for her family, and for those
whom she helps to combat the invasive disorder
that completely changed her life."*

*"Character cannot be developed in ease and quiet. Only through experiences of trial and suffering can the soul be strengthened, vision cleared, ambition inspired and success achieved."*

*-Helen Keller*

Imagine for a moment that you're a teenage girl, pretty and popular. You are the only daughter of two loving parents and the sister to a caring brother. You are a sophomore at a Christian based academy where you've been enrolled since kindergarten. You are a straight A student, as well as a member of the cheerleading squad, the band, the choir and the musical ensemble. You've also just finished playing the lead in your school's annual musical, singled out from among 500 members of the student body.

In short, you are the perfect All-American girl, living the perfect All-American life.

Now imagine that at the end of your sophomore year your parents explain that your father has earned a new job promotion. They tell you that you will soon be moving from your hometown of Dayton, Ohio to Lockport, New York where in September, you'll be enrolled in a public school of over four thousand students.

In short, your perfect All-American life is unraveling at the seams. Worse yet, there's nothing you can do to change it. You have absolutely no control.

Such is the early life story of Dawn Copperthite, a soft spoken 37-year old nutritional therapist who uses her talents to counsel women, men, and children trapped within the life-threatening web of eating disorders. Dawn developed the character and wisdom

essential to her counseling profession through the trials and
suffering she herself endured as a teenage anorexic.

"When my family moved, it was a terrible time for me,"
Dawn recalls with a quiet intensity. "I'd gone to the same small
school all of my life. I grew up with the kids in that school.
They all knew me, and the teachers all knew me. We had a dress
code and rules and I was comfortable there. When I transferred
to the public school in Lockport there were so many more kids.
They wore anything they wanted, and they pretty much did and
said anything they wanted. In every way, it was shocking to me
how different it was. And no matter what I did, I felt so out of
place."

Trusting her mother's reassurances
that she would eventually adapt to her
new environment, Dawn actively worked
at becoming more involved. She joined
the school band and went out for the
swim team. Yet the more she extended
herself, the more solitary her world
became. In short, Dawn found it almost
impossible to make new friends. Her
grades began slipping and she lost
interest in all extra curricular activities.

By March of 1985, the forlorn teen
was inescapably mired in a painful
existence that made her feel as if she
had no power over any part of her life.
Overwhelmed and distraught, Dawn
relates that she decided to embark
on a new course of action.

*Dawn, age 19, at the lowest
point of her anorexia battle
weighing only 90 pounds.*

"I went on a diet where I only ate healthy foods. Then, one by one, I started weeding out specific food groups until I was hardly eating anything. My weight dropped from 130 to 94 pounds, and I went from wearing size 10/12 clothes to a size zero, all within five months."

Following textbook anorexic behavior, Dawn cleverly hid her eating habits and her weight loss from family and friends while exposing conspicuous exercise routines.

"I started by using the Jane Fonda aerobics tape in the middle of the family room every night. I couldn't skip doing it, no matter what. Then that summer I moved on to walking every night for an hour and a half. Since I'd hardly eaten anything for months, when I finished my walk, I would be so exhausted that I couldn't go up the stairs at my house without my heart pounding as if it was going to explode outside of my chest. But by then, even when I wanted to eat, I couldn't."

By choosing not to eat Dawn believed she was reclaiming control of her floundering teenage life. What she didn't understand was that her diminished eating patterns would, in time, become mentally habit forming and eventually decimated her young body of every nutrient required for growth and survival. Finally her parents took stock of her unorthodox behaviors. They proactively organized a counseling intervention forcibly sent their daughter to a clinic specializing in the treatment of anorexia. Only then did Dawn truly begin to understand the scope of her illness.

"I was mad at my parents for making me go to the clinic, but I was also relieved. I wanted food, but my mind just wouldn't let me eat. I hoped that the clinic would be somewhere that I could feel safe and finally be able to eat again."

Dawn's struggle with her eating disorder lasted for ten years through high school, college, and into her adult life. On the positive side, the pain of Dawn's anorexic experience motivated her to pursue an educational degree in clinical dietetics at Buffalo State College. It was Dawn's hope that the degree would help her establish a career in the field of home and/or institutional food counseling. Her college experience, joined with the arrival of a kindred spirit in her life, paved the way for her recovery.

"I liked my classes but I hated dorming," Dawn states in recounting her college years. "I was still struggling with anorexia and hovering around 100 pounds, so I was too weak to even care for myself, no less for friends. So every weekend I went home."

As it turned out, Dawn wasn't the only one frequenting her family's Lockport home on weekends. Jamie Copperthite, a friend of her brother's, also started coming around with increasing regularity. Eventually he and a few friends began dropping by the Buffalo State Campus mid-week to spend time with Dawn. Finally this gentle man began making the trek on his own. Dawn's piercing blue eyes sparkle as she recalls those visits.

"Each time Jamie and I talked, I would tell him a little bit more about me until finally he knew it all. And I discovered that as long as I was with him, I could eat. He would order food and I would take bites off his plate or share and taste whatever he chose. It was the way that I learned to eat again and that it was okay to eat. Jamie was safe and he validated what I felt and who I was. He treated me like a human being, not like an eating disordered person."

*Dawn with her husband Jamie.*

Over the course of Dawn's college education, Jamie became her trusted friend and eventually her cherished fiancé. In June of 1992 the couple married and in December of 1995 Dawn gave birth to their first child, a daughter Renee Elizabeth, followed by a son, Bryan James in March of 1998. Dawn unequivocally states that her children were the final piece of her healthy life puzzle.

"While Jamie helped me put my life back on track, the birth of my children really gave me the incentive to stay healthy. Because of them, my life has become a journey of awareness."

As she became more aware of the eating disorder connection between body and mind, Dawn started to expand her professional reach outside the realm of traditional dietetic counseling. Invaluable post-graduate experience garnered in her early jobs at Park Ridge Community Hospital in Rochester, Sister's Hospital in Buffalo, and Lockport Memorial Hospital helped her step up to a whole new career level.

"I was hired as the Chief Dietician at The United Memorial Medical Center in Batavia and at about the same time I began my own private practice, counseling people with eating disorders. I was one of only two dietetic counselors in the Western New York area who could provide both body and mind counseling."

Within two years, Dawn's private practice expanded to the point that she was faced with a challenging choice. She had to either reduce her counseling services or resign from the Medical Center. After much prayer and thoughtful discussion with Jamie, on September 23, 2002 Dawn left the Medical Center and officially hung out her shingle as a full-time counselor. Despite the fact that her office hours were initially split between three different locations, Dawn notes with a quiet pride that her practice flourished.

"I had referrals coming out my ears, to the point that it was a little overwhelming. But it was also very rewarding in that people clearly wanted to come to me. They would keep coming back and we built relationships and you could see their progress."

The positive results Dawn achieved with her patients also earned her positive notice throughout the Western New York Medical Community. During the time she was building her reputation on a strong client base, and a solid referral trade, a Canadian businessman was building an eating disorder center on the outskirts of Williamsville. As Dawn details, it was only a matter of time before the two intersected.

"Art Boese is a father of three girls, all of whom struggled with eating disorders. In order to help those suffering as his daughters did, Art established The Avalon Eating Disorder Treatment Center in 1998, the only facility of its kind in Western New York. In February of 2004, the CEO of the Center contacted me. We met and he offered me the position of Nutrition Director, which I immediately accepted."

Dawn's continuing responsibilities at Avalon encompass patient counseling on nutrition education and individualized meal planning, along with awareness raising of the thoughts and emotions behind patient eating disordered behaviors. It's a job description custom made for the well-trained and personally experienced counselor.

"I'm not your average dietician. I don't just tell my patients what to eat. They don't come to in my office for a meal plan and leave. I want to know what happened in their life that triggered their eating problems and then help them to realize the value of that knowledge so they can keep it from happening again."

*Nailah Leftwich of Williamsville, Avalon client, with counselor Dawn Copperthite.*

Dawn finds that her counseling career is not only satisfying as a professional, it is also validating on a personal level. As she spends time with her patients eating crackers and homemade cookie snacks, preparing well balanced meals in the Avalon kitchen, sharing her personal anorexia experiences, and encouraging them to learn from their mistakes, she is reminded of the value of her own struggle.

"It's hard to put into words how you cannot want to eat," she explains. "In fact, it's almost inexplicable to someone who's never had an eating disorder. But I believe that I endured my eating disorder so that I could become more effective with what has become the purpose of my life, to help others."

When asked if she fears that her own children might follow in her anorexic path, Dawn acknowledges the possibility. "Research shows that there is a genetic predisposition to anorexia. It's just that people never get tested to find out. But my children maintain a healthy and active lifestyle and when they tell me they're full, they're full. I never force them to eat."

And what if they exhibited eating disorder signs? "I'd have them see another therapist, because I know kids have a tendency not to listen to their parents."

While Dawn's own children might not listen to her therapeutic wisdom, hundreds of Western New York eating disordered patients have survived and become healthy thanks to her counseling skills. It is a life that the once lost and lonely teenage girl could never have imagined, but one that this strong and capable woman now relishes and commands.

"I'm the best dietician there is for eating disorders because I've lived it, and because I can give them nutritional advice and therapy at the same time. But most importantly, just as Jamie did for me, I make my patients feel safe. Safe in their health habits and safe as people."

# Dawn's Fruit Salad

*"When I was really sick, this was about the only food that I would eat.
My mom would make it for me and I would eat it for breakfast and lunch,
so it's a very special recipe to me."*

*-Dawn Copperthite*

## INGREDIENTS

2 cans pineapple chunks

2 cans mandarin oranges

1 jar maraschino cherries, drained and halved

1 banana, sliced

2 packages tapioca pudding

## DIRECTIONS

• Drain and reserve liquid from pineapple and mandarin oranges.

• Prepare tapoica pudding using 3 cups of the reserved fruit liquid.

• Bring tapioca to boil stirring constantly.

• Remove pudding from heat and allow to cool.

• When cooled, combine pudding, pineapple, mandarin oranges, and
  halved cherries. Stir together and refrigerate.

• Add banana slices just before serving.

# Chicken Wing Wisdom V

*"We meet in one of Buffalo's trendy West Side Bars. She appears long and lean, with a hip haircut and chic clothes; outward signs of her elevated status as a world caliber business executive.*
*Yet when we speak of her life, her struggles, and her accomplishments, we are alike--wives, mothers, women, fighting the same battles and wishing the same dreams."*

*Don't be afraid of the space between your dreams and reality. If you can dream it, you can make it so.*

*-Belva Davis-Award Winning Journalist*

Nadja Piatka is a transplanted Western New York woman who clearly has no fear of the space between her dreams and reality. Over the last thirteen years the Canadian native has set and achieved personal goals that have transformed her into a highly successful businesswoman, a best selling author, a proven newspaper columnist, a seasoned television personality, and an in-demand public speaker. And she accomplished it all by the simple act of turning on her oven and baking.

"My parents were born in the Ukraine and they immigrated to Canada after World War II," Nadja states in explaining her baking background. "In time they purchased a greasy spoon restaurant in Sudbury, Canada where our family lived upstairs and where I fell in love with the food business. That devotion also caused me to become overweight during my teen years. So I began experimenting with recipes for myself, trying to create low fat/low calorie foods that tasted good."

In time, Nadja's cooking experiments morphed into a recipe collection that formed the tasty foundation for her internationally acclaimed Nadja Foods, wholesale supplier of healthy foods across the United States and Canada. Yet it's her innate sense of wisdom behind her entrepreneurial experience that tells her real story.

In 1992, Nadja was a traditional stay-at-home, suburban housewife and mother of two school age children. However, her picture perfect life skewed out of control the day her husband of twenty years suddenly and permanently walked out the door. As she recalls, the emotionally devastating turn of events left

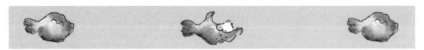

her debt-ridden, homeless, and, most frightening of all, completely responsible.

"My children and I moved into a small house on the 'wrong side of the tracks' in Edmonton where I spent my days trying to figure out how I was going to pay the bills."

During this time, one particularly ambitious debt collector actually came calling at Nadja's house. He walked around the outside and peered in windows, loudly yelling embarrassing insults including "deadbeat." Frightened, the protective mother grabbed her daughter and ducked under the kitchen table, hoping the collections agent would think no one was home.

"It was an awful experience for both of us," Nadja states. "But it was also a turning point in that I decided this kind of thing wasn't going to happen anymore."

When the bill collector finally gave up and left, Nadja crawled out from underneath the table and went in search of a piece of paper. In desperation, she grabbed a cardboard insert from a pair of panty hose. At the top she wrote the word, "goals." Underneath she wrote a list of six life objectives:

1) I will own an international company.
2) I will be a best selling author.
3) I will have my own newspaper column.
4) I will be a public speaker.
5) I will have my own TV Show.
6) I will bring value to people's lives.

Remarkably, within a year's time, the once distraught house-wife accomplished almost all of those goals, using her card-board list as daily inspiration.

"After I wrote that the list I figured I had nothing to lose. Once I came to that conclusion an unshakable belief, almost like providence, moved through me, and that's when I decided to survive."

Nadja formulated her survival on the thing she knew best. "I always liked baking, and by this time I was pretty good at creating foods that were low fat and tasted good. So I started getting up at 4 a.m. and baking low fat muffins to sell at bakeries and coffee shops in town."

*Nadja Piatka*

As providence would have it, consumer demand for Nadja's tasty baked goods quickly escalated. Increased sales encouraged the muffin maker to outsource the production of her healthy treats. That action, in turn, allowed Nadja to expand her horizons and develop other segments of her business.

She began writing a newspaper column on low fat cooking. She signed a contract to author a book entitled, *The Joy of Losing Weight*.

Regular appearances on Edmonton talk shows and public speaking engagements soon followed. Toward the end of her first year in business, Nadja formed a professional partnership with two Canadian businesswomen and from there, it was only a

short step to national prominence. Soon McDonald's of Canada hired the muffin maven to provide all of their restaurants with her low fat treats.

Infused with an entrepreneurial spirit, Nadja further extended her professional reach by organizing a series of women's get-away weekends. Using hotels in major Canadian cities such as Edmonton, Calgary, and Vancouver, Nadja focused the retreats on healthy foods and pampering spa treatments within the atmosphere of a weekend pajama party. She creatively afforded the upfront costs of each event by cross bartering.

"I could only create work for myself that didn't require capital investment. So I convinced the hotels to give a free weekend to the newspapers, who in turn promoted the event without charge. It ended up being a win-win situation for everyone."

As a result of her wide ranging success, five short years after a relentless bill collector publicly dubbed her a "deadbeat," Nadja Piatka was honored as a regional winner of the Canadian Woman Entrepreneur of the Year Award.

Quickly achieving her dreams encouraged the newly respected businesswoman to expand her list of goals. She penned another cookbook entitled, *The Outrageously Delicious Fat Wise Cookbook* and donated all the profits to The Ronald McDonald House. She licensed her low-fat muffin recipes to an International Food Company for a very healthy profit.

Most significantly, Nadja began experimenting with a new low fat recipe for chocoholics. Once she secured the formula, she officially christened the product, Nadja's Healthy Brownie. Then, in a familiar pattern, the resourceful baker used the low-fat treat to advance a whole new set of personal and professional dreams.

"When I came up with a brownie I thought was good enough, I took it to Dan Mohan, development agent for Subway Shops in Calgary. He gave me the chance to test it in his stores and within a year, Subway added the brownie to their menus all across Canada."

This sweet success in her homeland spawned a professional desire within Nadja to expand to the United States. In 1998 she attended a trade mission sponsored by the Canadian Department of Foreign Affairs and International Trade at Buffalo's Albright Knox Art Gallery. As it turned out, the seminar advanced her business as well as her personal life, directly into the Queen City.

*Nadja and Doug.*

"I met Doug at the trade seminar and it was love at first sight."

Nadja's expressive brown eyes warm in describing her initial encounter with current husband Doug Smith.

"Unfortunately after that seminar, between business and personal issues, we didn't see each other again for two years. But eventually we reconnected, started dating, and married on Valentine's Day, 2002."

Nadja's marriage dictated a move to her husband's hometown, which was fine with the new bride.

"I love Buffalo," she emphatically states. "The food is great and the people here are so warm and wonderful."

Nadja was also warmly welcomed on a national level as Americans quickly embraced her low fat foods. Within months of setting up shop in Buffalo, she signed a contract with the American Division of Subway Stores for rights to her healthy brownie, achieving yet another of her business dream goals of owning an international company. Though it wasn't until after the Subway deal was signed that her brownie bandwagon really started to roll.

One late Wednesday afternoon the phone in Nadja's office rang. It was a long distance call from Chicago. Oprah Winfrey's television producer was on the line. It seemed that a Subway Store was located across the street from Harpo Studios. Oprah tried Nadja's brownies and loved them. Now she wanted to meet the woman who'd created the wonderfully tasty, low fat treat. Could Nadja and her brownies be in Chicago the following week? Nadja immediately responded that anything Oprah wanted, she could provide.

"I'd been in touch with her staff once or twice about my brownies, but nothing ever came of it," the creative cook explains. "I guess Oprah just had to try them for herself!"

Four days after receiving the fortuitous phone call, a film crew began following Nadja around Buffalo, detailing her brownie-based empire for Oprah and her legion of viewers. Two days later, both baker and brownies were winging their way to Chicago, headed for what Nadja remembers as the experience of a lifetime.

"I wanted to be on the Oprah Show so badly, yet I was afraid that when I got on I was going to faint, or mess it up. But once I was with Oprah, it was great. She makes you feel like a girlfriend. She's really quite magical."

Since her American television debut, Nadja has continued to forge her dreams into realities. To date, Nadja's Brownies are sold in Subway Stores in 30 states, with 70% of her total business now centered in the United States. She estimates that her company currently produces 300,000 brownies a month.

Additionally, in 2005, she signed a contract with one of the world's largest foodservice companies, Sodexho, which services Western New York institutions such as M&T Bank, Buffalo State College and Niagara University. Under the agreement terms, the creative cook has developed new and tasty products such as Nadja's Petite Angel Cakes and Nadja's Muffins.

Most recently, the American Heart Association welcomed Nadja into their fold as a recipe developer and a board of director for their North East Affiliate. Together they are working on the advancement of healthy, yet flavorful, low fat foods. Further Nadja's low fat brownie has become an official lunch room offering in a number of Buffalo schools, with educational facilities across America preparing to follow the Queen City's lead. To promote her healthy food ideas Nadja has also become a regular guest on Buffalo and Rochester talk shows to discuss the topic of childhood obesity and the importance of healthy food.

Last but not least, Nadja's pajama party weekends are in full swing across Canada and have kicked off in the United States with a February, 2005 Caribbean Cruise Ultimate Pajama Party sailing from Ft. Lauderdale, Florida. All of which means that in the last 13 years Nadja has managed to reach and surpass every dream that she scribbled on her fabled piece of pantyhose cardboard and imagined in her mind.

So what could she possibly have left to achieve?

"I want to be on the cover of Forbes and People Magazines," Nadja states without hesitation. "I also want to keep working on my recipes. Re-inventing and improving some, and creating others. I'm always challenging myself to make them better and more healthy."

And what continues to inspire her dreams?

"When I was growing up my mother would always tell me that I was special and that I had a special connection to food. She had a lot of confidence in me and used to say that one day I would do it all. And I guess her words have stuck with me all of my life."

# Nadja's Oatmeal Chocolate Chip Cookies

*" My children have always enjoyed these cookies which are lower in fat and calories and higher in fiber that regular chocolate chip cookies."*

–*Nadja Piatka*

## INGREDIENTS

3/4 c. diet margarine

3/4 c. brown sugar

1/4 c. Splenda sugar substitute

3 egg whites

1/4 c. molasses

1 t. vanilla

1 c. all purpose flour

1 t. cinnamon

1 t. baking soda

2 1/2 c. quick cooking oats

3/4 c. semi-sweet chocolate chips

## DIRECTIONS

• Preheat oven to 350 F (180 C)

• Beat butter and sugars together.

• Add egg whites,molasses, and vanilla. Beat until smooth.

• In a seperate bowl stir together flour, salt, cinnamon, baking soda and oats

• Combine with butter mixture. Add chocolate chips.

• Drop rounded teaspoonfuls of dough 1 inch apart onto baking sheets sprayed with non-stick cooking spray.

• Bake for 10 to 12 minutes or until golden.

• Makes 50 cookies

Per cookie: 40 Calories 1.5 grams of fat.

# Chicken Wing Wisdom VI

*"Her unusual name offers an immediate indication of her unique person. She is a woman of traditional home values immersed in a non-traditional profession, both of which benefit from her proven cooking skills. She learned her craft at the hands of her mother and her grandmother, making her good taste in food seem almost innate. But her acknowledgment of true achievement in life comes when she speaks of her daughter, for whom she is working to change the world."*

*"Good taste [in cooking] is innate. It is knowing with certainty when and how to break the rules and when not to--- a talent few possess."*

*-Michael McLaughlin, famed cookbook author.*

In today's fast food world, we Americans hunger for creative taste sensations at every breakfast, lunch, and dinner we consume. In between our meals we search out the latest snack food fads and wash them down with trendy beverages guaranteed to quench our thirsts and cure our ills. So it comes as no surprise that the business of developing new foods delectable enough to please our palates and entice our wallets has grown into a billion-dollar enterprise.

Thirty-six year old Jude'th (Jude) Crisafulli stands front and center in the ever-evolving world of new foods a professional as a research and development (R&D) bakery scientist at Rich Products; a Western New York-based international food supplier and food solutions provider. After 13 years in Rich's employ Jude is well respected among her peers for the certainty of her innate R&D talents, which most recently have helped her guide the international food supplier in the development of low fat, healthy baked goods. She is a woman who knows when and how to break cooking rules, and when not to, and most essentially she is a woman who acquired her culinary talents the old fashioned way.

"My grandmother and my mother were the biggest influences over my cooking skills," Jude states. "My mother always had all of us kids in the kitchen cooking with her, including my brothers. She would give us each jobs to do and mine was always making gravy. I had fun playing around with it, adding this and that, and perfecting it. Even now when my family gets together it's still my job to make the gravy and I still love trying to perfect it. "

Growing up in South Buffalo, Jude's youthful interests were so focused on cooking that as a teenager she decided to pursue a degree at Buffalo State College in the culinary field. It was Jude's belief that by achieving a higher education in food she would provide a foundation for her dream of one day owning her own restaurant or bakery.

In 1991, after earning a Bachelors of Science in food service management, Jude began her professional career as a part time dietary supervisor at a local nursing home, and also as a cook in the Air Force Reserves. Yet it was only a matter of months before Jude interviewed for what she believed would be the job of her dreams, associate director of food services at a Rochester based hospital.

At the time, Jude was living at home, sharing the nighttime care of her ailing grandmother with her sister, Madelyn. However as she progressed through her "dream job" interview, Jude came to the realization that it would be unfair to move to Rochester and leave her sister with sole care of their grandmother every night. So, reluctantly, she withdrew her application.

"I really wanted that job," Jude states with a lingering wistfulness. " But I knew it wouldn't have been right to leave my sister alone with my grandmother. So, I prayed to St. Jude and told him that since I'd done the right thing, he had to hook me up." With a bright smile she tells of her prayerful response.

"Around an hour later I got a phone call from Rich's about a job application I'd submitted. And the rest is history."

While Jude acknowledges that the Rich's phone call was a possible coincidence, she declares that her strong devotion to the Catholic Saint for whom she is named is based on a miraculous reality.

Jude reverentially tells the story of her mother, Kathaleen, who was diagnosed with a tumor in her fallopian tubes while pregnant with her seventh child. Doctors gave the expectant woman two choices: terminate the pregnancy or die. Being a faithful Catholic, Kathaleen decided to continue the pregnancy. Medical experts subsequently forecasted that if by some miracle the baby should make it to full term, the child would never be born "normal."

Facing that traumatic medical prognosis, Kathaleen prayed to St. Jude, the Patron Saint of Impossible Causes. She promised that if he would ensure her baby's healthy survival, she would honor the miracle by christening the child with his name.

The happily ever after ending is that, on January 30, 1969, Jude'th Crisafulli was born lively and strong. Even more amazing was that Kathaleen's tumor miraculously stopped growing during the remainder of her pregnancy. After giving birth, doctors performed a partial hysterectomy and the faithful mother of seven went on to enjoy a long and still healthy life.

When asked if her unusual name ever served as a liability rather than a blessing, Jude answers with a gentle pride. "I always understood the reason my mother named me outweighed any price I had to pay."

Following her serendipitous hiring, Jude began her Rich's R &D career as a 1st Level Bakery Technician. Her initial duties involved working with a technologist and a scientist on the creation of Russian Black Bread and butter croissants. Yet Jude's obvious talents encouraged Rich's Management to advance her responsibilities to independent projects, each assignment more fully expanding the novice researcher's knowledge of food development.

*Jude at work at Rich Products food labratories.*

"It was a lot different making things at Rich's than it was at home," Jude states with a knowing laugh. "I quickly found out that in research and development, food is as much about science as it is about creativity. I had to learn about the functionality of the ingredients and how they interact. It was really a big learning curve for me."

Jude's taste talents helped her to quickly navigate that scientific food curve. In 1995 she was promoted to food technician level 2, with job responsibilities solely focused on independent projects. Her solo work involved researching appropriate, and innovative ingredients and or processes essential to the creation of a successful food product. Next she would undertake a trial and error formulation through which she would produce an actual food sample. Jude would then present her sample product to the Rich's marketing department and, based on their feedback, she would either return to the kitchen for modifications, or move on to a consumer panel for sensory testing.

"When I began working on solo projects I really began to acquire my own product development styles," Jude recalls. "Going through trial and error to create products is what really allowed me to build a larger data base in my brain regarding ingredient functionalities, equipment, and operational resources."

Jude excelled at her new job responsibilities and enjoyed the challenges of the work. Yet within two years of her promotion she experienced a life-changing event that diverted her professional focus and almost stymied her professional R&D success. It was a blessed event in the form of a pink bundle of joy named Maria.

In 1997 with the birth of her daughter, Jude decided to reduce her work hours to part time. Despite the cutback, Jude proficiently maintained her above average work ethic, to the extent that Rich's offered her a promotion to the advanced level of Food Technologist. There was, however, one condition to her advancement: Jude had to return to work as a full time employee. After negotiating a somewhat flexible work schedule and relying on the employee benefit of Rich's in-house day care, Jude agreed.

"The day care center was located just outside my office so I could bring Maria with me to work everyday and see her whenever I wanted," Jude recalls. "So even though I was hesitant at first, it really worked out well."

*Jude with daughter Maria at her kindergarten graduation*

The step-up to food technologist meant the continued handling of her own food development projects as well as off-site meetings with clients who custom ordered the foods. Suddenly, Jude found herself doffing her white lab coat and leaving behind Rich's savory test kitchen to attend corporate board meetings with representatives of international and nationally known chain restaurants, supermarkets, and quick service eateries. To her delight, Jude discovered that time spent outside the lab enhanced her research.

"Meeting customers face to face really helped me develop baked good recipes for the exact cookie or muffin or bread they wanted. I could stand next to the customer and listen to their voice explain the specific size they had in mind, how they were going to serve it, where it would be displayed, where it would be stored, all the information about the product that would make them happy and make it work for their operation. Those are the details that you never know back in the kitchen, but which make such a difference in the product's creation."

Jude's ability to successfully balance the creation of new foods along with the added element of client interaction encouraged Rich's Management to again move Jude up the corporate ladder. In short order she was promoted to Food Technologist Level 1 followed by another direct corporate advancement to Senior Food Technologist. The bonus to Jude's progression was that the increased amount of research required in each new post led her to a new and exciting area of advanced food development.

"In my job at Rich's I've pretty much worked on developing cookies and muffins so I'm always doing research on baked goods," Jude states. "In the last few years I've been reading more and more about the trans fatty acids traditionally used in those foods and the damage they inflict. The more I read, the more I started thinking that there had to be a better way, so I started figuring out how to create healthier products."

Jude's timing perfectly coincided with that of Rich's top executives, already working on plans to reduce trans fat in their prepared foods. It was only a matter of time before the international corporation assigned Jude her first low trans fat task.

"I was given the project of developing a muffin with zero grams of trans fat, which is really tough to do. Partially hydrogenated oil gives muffins volume and their soft crumb texture. If you eliminate that fat and use others, then the saturated fat count goes up, which is another problem. On top of flavor and texture, I also have to be concerned with using our existing equipment to create the muffin, as well as keeping the price around the same cost as our other baked goods."

When asked if the task offered an impossible objective, Jude confidently answers, "I never say that I can't do something. I always feel that you can accomplish almost anything if you have

enough time. It's just a matter of doing the research and putting in the time."

According to Jude's experience, the length of time required to develop a food product can vary anywhere from weeks to years. She notes that, as in any baking process, it all begins with a recipe. That recipe may come from Rich's existing files or from a variety of other sources including, on occasion, employees' own family formulas. From that point, the ingredients are tweaked to meet the specific product need.

Once a well-researched sweet formulation is perfected, it is then delivered in taste samples to company executives and to the client. This step may take place a number of times until all agree that the product has the exact flavor, texture and quality desired.

Next, the big hurdle of transferring the product from the sterile and controlled atmosphere of Rich's test kitchen into a looming production plant is tackled. Rich's maintains food factories in Virginia and Tennessee where products are produced in thousand pound quantities. When a new food finally passes the daunting large-scale factory test, then all systems are go.

Jude proudly states that after months of focused work, she was able to achieve her assigned recipe task for a zero grams trans fat muffin. The process has encouraged the creative food scientist to undertake additional healthy food development, which will undoubtedly continue to provide better food products for Rich's International client base. Yet from Jude's perspective, her pledge to healthier foods is more closely grounded and per-sonally relevant.

"All of the research I've done on this project has really made me think about good health and the food I'm putting in my body everyday. And the fact that I have a daughter makes a difference too. Because of Maria I've made it my goal to create healthier products geared toward children. Foods lower in sugars and fats and higher in fiber that children will still enjoy."

As a valuable byproduct of her healthy food research, Jude has become a valued trans fat solution expert in the Rich's test kitchen. She is also a product developer sought out by her peers for help and advice. It's a professional role she characterizes as exciting and challenging

"I love to troubleshoot, especially if it's a product that I haven't developed. I'm really passionate about my work when I'm fixing something, getting in there and mixing and figuring out what will make it better. In fact, after all these years, when a product is in the oven, I still get butterflies watching and waiting to see if my solution works."

Jude collaborates on her R&D solutions with a staff comprised of men and women alike. From her perspective, gender definitely plays a role in approaches to product development.

"Women sit and discuss the food, sharing it, and even bringing in their grandmother's recipes to help make improvements. I find that it's a lot like the women in my family who taught me to cook, they develop food with a sense of love."

From her professional actions and attitudes, it's obvious that Jude undertakes her R&D work with a genuine sense of love and devotion. At the same time, she quietly nurtures future plans outside the world of food development. She has written a children's book about a parent who spends time away from home on business trips. She is in the middle of scripting her first novel, which she classifies as an "historical romance." And she still quietly dreams about owning her own restaurant or bakery. Yet this accomplished woman passionately declares that her professional aspirations pale when compared to her roles as daughter, wife, and mother.

"Nothing else is as important to me as my family. I think that I'm truly happiest when I am with them."

Check with her all-important family and they will profess that Jude can whip up a variety of taste tempting meals including Chicken French ala Jude, a free form concoction of chicken, spinach, rice and white wine which is her husband Mark's favorite. Consult her co-workers at Rich's and they will confirm that Jude is an innately talented food researcher, developer, and consultant. Yet ask Jude to self assess her cooking abilities, and she confesses a belief that she is a poor imitation of the real thing.

"Any of my mother's recipes that I make, you just can't beat. There is nothing I can to do to improve on her food. She's just the best cook in the world."

Then pausing to collect her thoughts, Jude unassumingly acknowledges the wisdom of the significant food contributions she has made in her research and development career.

"It does make me happy to think that someone could be having a bad day anywhere and then eat one of my cookies or muffins, and all of a sudden, it's better. I've made a difference in their day and they're happier. To me that's the most important thing about my work --- that what I do makes people happy"

## Jude's Low Fat Lemon Strawberry Cake

*"This has become one of my favorite dessert recipes.
I like it because it's healthy in that it's lower in fat and has fruit in it.
And it's light and refreshing...especially on a hot summer day."*

*—Jude Crisafulli*

### INGREDIENTS

1 box (2 layer) lemon cake mix
1 (12oz.) can diet 7-up or ginger ale
1 1/2 to 2 cups fresh/frozen strawberries
Lite whipped topping

### DIRECTIONS

• Mix cake and soda together and pour batter into a 13 x 9 inch baking pan.

• Evenly drop the berries over the top of the batter.

• Bake according to package instructions.

• Top with whipped topping to serve.

• This cake can be served both warm and cold. It's delicious either way.

Note: If you are on a weight watchers diet, cut the cake into 15 portions and it will be 3 points per serving.

# Chicken Wing Wisdom VII

*"She's blond and sassy with a non-stop conversational style that allows for only one short breath between her next run-on sentence. Her body is a bundle of energy that swoops up anyone even remotely interested in her healthy lifestyle crusade. She offers advice, information, and nutritive wisdom in a full-out enthusiasm to those seeking her counsel. She is, in a way, a performer always seeking to teach through her creatively entertaining ways. Yet as the window to her soul, her eyes reveal the tender nature of her character and the depth of her personal wounds - wounds that she has remarkably formulated into her own style of Chicken Wing Wisdom."*

*"Turn your wounds into wisdom."*

*-Oprah*

How does a self-described "fat and introverted" teenage girl from Long Island transform into a slender, personable, and in-demand nutrition educator, wellness coach, and motivational speaker?

In Sharon Lawrence's case, her metamorphosis evolved as she turned her personal wounds into wisdom---Nutritional Dynamics wisdom.

The five-foot-eight inch, 125 pound, healthy lifestyle guru is the founder and owner of Nutrition Dynamics, a Western New York based wellness company that she began in 1991. Sharon states that her purpose in developing the business was to "educate, motivate and empower" people to take charge of their health, much as she once did.

"As a young girl, I had terrible self esteem issues. I didn't socialize much, I had poor grades and I never felt as beautiful, intelligent or talented as my older sister. My perceived inadequacy often compelled me to hide out in my room, secretly consuming mass quantities of peanut butter and Oreo cookies. As a result, I was a big, fat kid who couldn't ride a bike, climb trees, run or even play with other kids at the park."

Her sister's departure for college lightened Sharon's self-esteem burden, which encouraged the young teen to undertake a remarkable self-improvement turn-around. She lost weight, became a straight A student, and started making friends. Unfortunately, one of those new-found friends was tragically killed in an alcohol related car accident. In response, Sharon became actively involved in a drug and alcohol awareness campaign at her high school. There she

learned the connection between mental, physical and spiritual health and an individual's overall well being. As she recalls, the revelation was purposeful.

"From that high school initiative I learned that by studying health I could impact people's lives in a dynamic and positive way. It also helped me to identify that helping people through health and wellness was what I wanted to do with my life."

To achieve her life's plan, Sharon pursued a nutrition degree at Buffalo State College and a related internship at the UCLA Veteran's Administration Wadsworth Hospital Center in Los Angeles, California. Upon graduating, her educational credentials immediately earned Sharon employment as a staff clinical dietitian at the Medical College of Virginia and later at Buffalo's Veteran's Administration (VA) Hospital. At the VA Sharon was recognized for Outstanding Achievement by the Chief of the Department of Medicine for her significant clinical contributions to the medical center - the first dietitian to ever be so honored.

*Sharon Lawrence at age 11*

Yet in counter balance to her professional accomplishments during these years, Sharon was personally struggling with a body weight fluctuating like a runaway roller coaster. From 1971 to 1978, she gained and lost as much as 65 pounds at a time. Her losses were always accomplished through fad dieting and her gains directly attributable to her life long habits of excessive eating and lack of exercise. But in 1979, the over-weight nutritionist came to a personal weight loss turning point.

Sharon was physically at the high end of her poundage pendulum, weighing in at about 190 pounds. She was working as a clinical dietitian, specializing in nutritional support for patients dealing with heart disease. Following one particular session, Sharon overheard her patient talking to his wife while waiting for the elevator. He was laughing over the fact that the nutritionist, who was supposed to teach him how to lose weight and maintain healthy blood pressure levels, was so overweight herself.

"The more he laughed, the harder I cried, " Sharon recalls, "What he said was true and I realized that as long as I was heavy, I had no credibility at all with my patients. So I decided right there, on the spot, to never go on another diet again. Instead I promised myself that I would find a way to eat healthy and permanently lose the weight. I was so lucky that I heard that man that day. He changed my life."

It took Sharon more than a year to shed 65 excess pounds from her delicate frame, using a solid methodology of healthy foods, portion control, exercise, stress management, self encouragement and laughter. Her physical reformation inspired the slimmed down educator to become more creative in her counseling sessions with patients. It also stimulated her to create a lecture series for the Mended Hearts Association, a group of cardiac surgery survival patients and families that regularly met at the VA Hospital. In time, her well-received weight loss message encouraged lecture requests from other community groups and she was invited to serve as a consultant to Sisters Hospital in their weight management program.

While Sharon's lectures were definitely compelling, they were not the sole reason that people were drawn to her presentations. It was her delivery style that equally captivated and entertained audiences. Flashing like an electric current

*Sharon Lawrence*

across the stage, launching her arms as pliant exclamation points, regulating her voice as an enthusiasm generator, Sharon could draw audience members in and make them feel like integral partners in her can-do world.

However, the dynamic lecturer unabashedly admits that public speaking was not always her strongest point.

"During the first three weeks of my internship at UCLA, I was required to deliver a nutrition workshop to fellow students and patients at the hospital's out-patient clinic. When I finished the presentation, the intern director took me into her office and informed me that my lecture was the worst she'd ever heard in her professional career.

She said that I talked at the students, using exceedingly large words they couldn't understand. She said that I was aloof and boring to watch, and that I didn't give those in attendance one simple concept to remember. Then she gave me an 'F' for the assignment and told me that if I didn't improve she was going to throw me out."

Despite her stinging evaluation, the director offered to help the lagging student improve her monotonous style and delivery. Through the use of videotaped rehearsals and continued critiques, the once boring and remote lecturer became electric. At graduation, her educational mentor proudly acknowledged Sharon as one of the best educators UCLA had ever produced.

As a boost to her well-learned teaching talents, Sharon amassed technical experience through employment in the late 1980s with Merck Pharmaceuticals. In her role as one of Merck's cardiovascular specialist representatives, Sharon expanded her medical knowledge, particularly in the areas of heart disease prevention and treatment. The increased knowledge proved equally valuable on a personal level as Sharon was able to advise her father, who suffered a number of heart attacks and strokes. Overall, the experience provided Sharon with an important prescriptive lesson, to which she still adheres, some fifteen years later.

"I worked with patients whose lives were turned around by the drugs we sold. But while watching my father endure the horrendous side effects from prescriptions he was given for his heart condition, I began to research herbal and nutraceutical alternative treatments. What I discovered in my studies formed the basis of the health and wellness precepts that I tell my clients today, that drugs should be prescribed only when necessary, not used blindly as preventative measures."

In 1991, Sharon took the wisdom of her wide-ranging medical knowledge along with her charismatic lecture style and structured them into a health and wellness business plan. She then partnered with friend Corinne Giannini, and each contributed $1000 in seed money to launch Nutrition Dynamics from a small office space on Niagara Falls Boulevard.

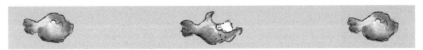

The duo's first professional endeavor involved a creative collaboration with area HMOs and Tops Supermarkets that they entitled "Supermarket Safari." The concept was simple. Consumers would travel with registered dietitian "guides" through the supermarket "jungle" where they would learn about "dangerous" high fat/high calorie foods and "safe" healthy food alternatives. The tours would then conclude with a sampling of nutritious foods. As Sharon notes, the safaris were an instant hit.

"We realized early on that consumers will buy "healthy foods" only if they taste wonderful and fit perfectly into their lifestyles. So we created the safaris to empower shoppers to find those healthy, great tasting foods, and it worked perfectly!"

As a means of extending their community outreach, Sharon and Corinne presented their healthy safari concept to Blue Cross and Blue Shield of WNY. Executives of the HMO loved the idea and immediately endorsed the program as an approved health prevention option for all of their subscribers. That action greatly increased demand for the healthy food tours, as subscribers were able to "safari" as part of their health insurance coverage plan. Yet as rapidly as Nutrition Dynamics was expanding, it was also changing.

"Although the business was getting stronger, we were not generating enough money to support two families," Sharon recalls. "So in 1994, Corinne decided it was time to move on. That same year, I contracted with Wegman's Food Markets to offer the Supermarket Safari Tours in their chain of stores. Their corporate commitment to providing healthy food options for consumers completely aligned with my nutritional vision and, as it turned out, it was a perfect marriage for us both."

Sharon's newly formed supermarket connection highlighted a number of nutritional needs that her existing health and wellness programs were not meeting. People enrolled in the Wegman's tours wanted to know how to go out to dinner or attend parties and maintain healthy eating habits. They wanted to know how to use healthy ingredients without "ruining" their favorite recipes. They begged for tips on handling coffee and chocolate cravings and late night TV snacking. They wanted how-to information and they wanted Sharon to provide it.

And so, *Lite'n Up* was born.

Responding to clients requests, Sharon and her team of dietitians formulated a comprehensive, twelve-week weight management and wellness program. They entitled it *"Lite'n Up!"* using the tag line description, "for optimum weight, health and vitality."

As she'd done before, Sharon pitched the program to Community Blue. Based on positive feedback the insurance provider had received about her supermarket safaris, the HMO execs immediately agreed to become program sponsors. Only this time, as Sharon notes, they weren't the only ones to jump on her wellness bandwagon.

*Sharon Lawrence*

"Within a year's time, Traditional Blue, Senior Blue, Univera Health Care and Senior Choice all became sponsors, allowing *Lite'n Up* to become a community wide offering. To deal with the increased demand, I expanded my team with additional registered dietitians, certified nutritionists, chefs, and stress and fitness specialists. At the same time, I continued to lecture on nutrition and wellness topics at corporations, schools, medical offices, and professional associations and began offering personal one-on-one nutritional counseling as well."

Sharon followed up the debut of *Lite'n Up!* with single session health and wellness workshops, luring clients with catchy titles such as Dashboard Dining, Be A Fat Detective, For Women Only! How to Survive the Holidays and Still Fit In Your Pants!, Super Foods, Guts, Butts and Go Nuts! Dis-Stress is Drivin' Me Crazy! And Nature's Remedy – The Power of Herbs.

The sassy branding of the classes along with the valuable nutritive lessons they offered turned the workshops into adult education mainstays throughout Western New York. They also catapulted Nutrition Dynamics into the forefront of wellness instruction at schools, corporations, hospitals and churches from Rochester, to Erie, Pennsylvania. In addition, Sharon's employee wellness programs and corporate retreats became popular and valued with businesses and professional associations.

"I knew there was a need out there," Sharon states. "And that became even more evident when our programs expanded without any outside marketing. By our fourth year in business, our classes were filling solely through word of mouth."

The word of mouth often heard when people talk about Nutrition Dynamics is "fun." Whether strolling through supermarkets, learning how to cook "lite," de-stressing and exercising, or sitting one-on-one discussing their individual needs, clients love the information they receive and the pro-active health regimen they are encouraged to begin and maintain. It's an inspirational combination powered directly through Sharon's energetic and enthusiastic outlook.

"You have to make it fun for people to participate," Sharon passionately states. "And I've found that the key is to encourage people to show up for life. Too many people I stand next to are dead from the waist up. I encourage them to become active participants in their lives, to be there mentally, physically and spiritually. Once that happens then they can't help but move forward."

Since beginning Nutrition Dynamics, Sharon's passion for helping people "show" up for life has helped more than 50 corporations and over ten thousand individuals move forward to improved health and wellness. It has also propelled her into key professional roles as a faculty member, official spokesperson and board member of eight Western New York organizations and a keynote speaker for groups and gatherings across Western New York and the United States. A core element of her appealing success is that her nutritional wisdom is based on simple,common sense directives to which people can easily relate.

"I tell people when they go to a party, instead of sitting next to the chips on the table at the end of the couch, to sit in the middle of the couch so that their fingers won't do the walking into that bowl. I tell them to turn their back to the bar so the hors d'ouerves won't be like a siren screaming their name! I remind them that a half hour before going to a party they need to munch on a high fiber snack to control their blood sugar, so the little food monster inside them won't jump out and eat everything at the party that's not nailed down. But most importantly, I teach them that it's the simple things that they do,

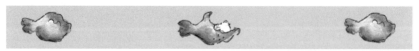

the little things. Anyone can do a big thing like diet for three weeks and then give up. It's the little things people do over time that really make the biggest difference."

Making a difference in people's lives is what Sharon Lawrence is all about. In her career as a nutrition educator she has achieved professional success and public acclaim. She has also faced unprincipled business dealings and related economic downturns that once forced her to sell her home and dictated several relocations of her business. Yet through it all, and despite continuing battles for economic balance, Sharon's "wounds to wisdom" mantra of helping others has never changed.

"There is a reason why I'm here. It's because I have a gift. I can take people by the hand and move them along, show them they can they live healthier lives, encourage them not to give up on themselves. I know in my own life, I've been blessed with three loyal, empathetic and compassionate women in my mother, my sister and my daughter who have all inspired me and helped me to keep going. So I understand how important that support can be. And when I see that light bulb turn on in someone, when they enjoy a healthier life because I've helped them not give up, it gives me a reason to get up in the morning. I know that I may be a catalyst and a change agent, but I'm also a friend, a warm soul who actually cares."

# Sharon's Amaretto Fruit Dip

*"I chose this wonderful recipe because it is filled with protein and very low in calories and fat and just might get people to eat more fruit. It is delicious served with any variety of fruit."*

-*Sharon Lawrence*

## INGREDIENTS

2 c. Lowfat Friendship Cottage Cheese

3/4 c. sifted powdered sugar

7 oz. light cream cheese

1 t. almond extract

1/2 fresh pineapple

decorative tooth picks

fresh mint leaves (optional)

## DIRECTIONS

• Place all ingredients except pineapple in container of electric blender and process until smooth, scraping as needed. Cover and chill.

• Create pineapple boat by carefully cutting out interior of fruit. Set boat aside.

• Cut fresh pineapple into 1" chunks.

• Pour cottage cheese mixture into pineapple boat.

• Center pineapple boat on a large platter and surround with pineapple chunks.

(As decorative option, place a toothpick in each pineapple chunk and decorate outer edges of pineapple with mint leaves.)

## NUTRITION FACTS: Per 1 T of dip

Calories 24, Total Fat 0.8 g, Saturated Fat 0.4 g, Total Carbohydrate 2.3 g, Protein 1.6 g, Cholesterol 3.0 mg, Sodium 45 mg, Fiber 0 g

# Chicken Wing Wisdom VIII

*"It was the best of times and the worst of times.
I was thrilled that my daughter's professional
accomplishments made her a likely profile for my
first book. However, after 25 years as a professional
journalist, I was unsure exactly how to go about
interviewing my own child. As we worked through
the process, I sensed my daughter's own uncertainty.
We both were so tentative in our questions and
answers, in contrast to our usual rapid-fire
mother-daughter banter. Unlike the rest, my
daughter's interview took longer to conduct and
much longer to write---three completely separate
versions on top of multiple smaller edits.
In the end though, we were both reasonably
satisfied--and much more aware of each other as
independent women connected by
a life line of food."*

*Food, after all, is not merely a product. It is necessary to our sustenance. Food is the support of life and is the center of the way we live when we take a moment to sit down and share life, share conversation, and share joy. That is the joy of cooking, which is a cliche, and yet is it the ultimate way we really fulfill ourselves and those around us.*

*- Piero Selvaggio-award winning restaurateur*

She sits curled upon her living room sofa, earnestly discussing the ideal of food as much more than life-sustaining nourishment. In between thoughts, she caringly attends to feeding her healthy, newborn child.

I sit across from her on the same couch, struggling to balance my roles of objective interviewer and proudly devoted mother. As I watch my daughter use her long, graceful fingers to interchangeably soothe her son and pinpoint her resolute words, my journalist's objectivity becomes further distracted by associated memories she recalls.

Lovingly packed brown bag school lunches, winter afternoon baking fests, family dinners spiced with lively conversation, holiday traditions flavored by specially prepared meals, precious life moments savored over favorite foods.

When I am finally able to disengage from our shared food memories and refocus on the interview at hand, I realize that my daughter's strong belief in her expanded food theory has become the basis of her life's philosophy. To be exact, my first-born child believes that food nourishes the mind and the soul as well as the body. That it is one of the ultimate ways in which we fulfill ourselves, and those around us. Simply put, in many ways and for many reasons, my daughter believes that life is all about food.

To her credit, my child has taken her strong personal food ideals and transferred them into her professional field where she is known and respected as Williamsville South High School English Teacher, Lisabeth Abt Pieters.

It was eight years ago that Lisa devised her High School Senior Elective aimed at teaching students the value of food in its varied aspects through reading and writing. As she acknowledges, the creative process was one that she truly relished.

*Mrs. Pieters in her "Food For Thought" classroom.*

"Over the years I had taught electives on travel writing, mystery writing, speech and communication, creative writing, and music journalism," Lisa states. "But in 1997, I decided that I wanted to create a new course, drawing on my personal food ideals and my own related experiences as an independent caterer and restaurant banquet manager."

Lisa formulated the class by referencing various curriculums she had studied through the course of her master's education and from national professional conferences in Nashville and Chicago. She also brainstormed with her fellow teachers. When, at last, she compiled a course of study, she then began assembling lists of books, writing assignments, activities, and films to serve as the elective's educational foundation.

Throughout her research and planning, Lisa made sure that the innovative elective completely fulfilled New York State Standards of reading, writing, listening, and speaking. At the same time, she was certain that the class' ultimate appeal would be much more universal, as she notes with a lilting laugh, "Everybody loves to eat!"

Once the curriculum variables were complete, the only missing element was the course title, which Lisa cleverly dubbed, *Food For Thought*.

The official introduction to *Food For Thought* is a student review of newspaper and magazine articles concerning the broad spectrum of approaches to food. When the overview is complete, students are assigned a reflective composition on the meaning of food in their lives.

In the next stage, Lisa provides her pupils with a list of food-related literature for required reading. Titles include such well known works as *Tender at the Bone, Miriam's Kitchen, Under the Tuscan Sun, Dinner at the Homesick Restaurant, Fried Green Tomatoes,* and *Like Water for Chocolate.* The students' reading task is followed by quizzes, discussions and an assigned research paper on a food-related subject.

Along with the varied reading and writing assignments, Lisa also requires the pupils to perform individual food presentations.

"The students have to choose a food that, for whatever reason, has meaning to them. They then have to make the dish, bring it to school and share it with the class. They also have to write an essay, to be read aloud in class, explaining why the food is significant."

Over and above the obvious appeal of being allowed to eat food in the classroom, Lisa explains that students often find this segment of the curriculum most rewarding.

"This is where it all comes together, where the kids finally get it," she states with an ardent enthusiasm. "Many times they choose a food that requires cooking with their families and then they bring their dish into school and share it with their class-mates. You can just see the light bulb go on as they begin to understand that food represents many different things in life. I love seeing that happen and I really remember those moments."

Some of Lisa's most memorable *Food For Thought* moments include the story of a student whose family maintains a cultural custom of making ravioli. To prepare for his presentation, the young man and his twin sister spent a Saturday with their grandparents, watching and learning how to mix and fill the delicate pasta pockets. The grandparents were so thrilled that they framed their grandson's presentation essay and hung it on their dining room wall. They also wrote Lisa a note expressing gratitude for her encouragement of their grandchildren's new found interest in their family's heritage.

Another favored moment involves a young girl's summer tradition of strawberry picking and jam making with her family. Not only was the student's fruit topping a delicious classroom treat, the essay she wrote about her family's seasonal ritual was tasty enough to be published in a local Western New York Magazine.

Lisa also treasures the tale of a foreign exchange student from Germany who called home for a recipe only to find it was written in metric measurements. Preparation of the dish became a transcontinental affair as both German and American families worked to formulate the required conversions.

And last but not least, Lisa lightheartedly recalls the story of the teen who lived near a McDonalds Restaurant. In his essay, the young man explained how he would regularly sneak out of the house for Egg McMuffins, much to the delight of his classmates who were enjoying their Golden Arches treats.

When asked if she believes that her food course achieves the objective of an English class, Lisa answers without hesitation.

"Yes, it meets all academic objectives and, in addition, it truly engages the students, which at this age can be difficult."

After a moment of thoughtful consideration, she adds, "When I first began teaching the course, it was definitely challenging. Students would walk into the classroom asking, 'When do we eat?' thinking that they didn't have to do anything. It took a while for them to understand that it was a legitimate course and that they would have to work." Lisa also proudly notes that once students got the message, the quality of their work soared.

"Over the years, students in this class turned in some of their best writing. And I think that's mainly due to the fact that the subject allows for heartfelt reflection, imagery and sensory detail, not only in the written assignments, but also in the food presentation. The kids get to smell, touch, and taste the food. It's a complete circle of sensory experiences."

Lisa notes that on occasion, *Food For Thought* has also provided her with some unsettling moments.

"Growing up in my family, we always sat down every night and ate dinner together and that was important to me. Conversely, what I've generally learned from student reflections is that most of the kids don't eat meals with their families, if they even have a complete family left. I've realized too that there is no thought about families coming together for food. The kids often eat alone, or with their friends."

On the bright side, as the course has progressed, more and more students have experienced personal "light bulb moments" that have allowed Lisa to witness her food elective making a difference.

"It's been poignant to watch, really. Since this is a senior year elective, the course comes at a time when teens are going through a total life change, so they are often reflective

*Lisa with her son Bennett.*

anyway. But as they go through the class they start to realize how much food means to them, not just as nutrition, but in connection with the people in their lives, their relationships, and their memories. And as with the young man making ravioli with his grandparents, they begin to see life differently and they change."

At the end of each "Food For Thought" session, Lisa undertakes a project that keeps the spirit of the curriculum alive. She publishes a cookbook of all the recipes so that the students and their families can share in the experience. The simply bound publication makes for mouth-watering reading with recipes such as Sweet Potato Pie, Summer Steak Salad, Grandma's Homemade Chicken Soup, and Aunt Lo's Famous Macaroni and Cheese. The tempting titles also raise the question if "Food For Thought" has ever experienced a food flop?

"Everyone's food always turned out," Lisa responds with a kind smile and a forgiving attitude. "A few kids blew off the assignment and did something silly like bringing crackers or a stick of butter which, to their surprise, made the others in the class mad. But overall it was a great success!"

While Lisa's strong belief in the ties that connect food and essential life experiences served as the inspiration for *Food For Thought*, it also recently encouraged the new mom to take a leave of absence from the teaching job that so clearly fulfills her professional life. These days instead of feeding high school students' minds, she is attending to the care and feeding of her own child's needs, thereby bringing her personal life philosophy full circle.

"I always knew how important food was nutritionally, in the way it makes us feel and helps our brains function, and socially as a means of connecting people through their traditions, and significant life events. But since the birth of my son, I've come to realize the enormous responsibility of food. My child can only eat what I give him. Therefore his mental and physical development is directly connected to whatever I choose to feed him. How he grows and the food preferences he will have for the rest of his life are being formed with every food I put on his plate. All of which has confirmed and clarified my food beliefs and made them so much stronger."

While Lisa builds and strengthens her food beliefs as a new mother, her *Food For Thought* elective is still being taught at Williamsville South High School. She acknowledges personal satisfaction that the unique curriculum is continuing to stimulate fresh new appetites in students, advancing a new level of understanding in a generation bereft of old fashioned food values. And as she sits curled on her living room sofa with her own child, she reflects on the overall significance of her food based elective, sharing a wisdom that reaches beyond the world of chalkboards and textbooks.

"Anyone who is an active participant in "Food for Thought" ends up reflecting not only on food, but on the memories and the personal relationships attached and I don't think that they ever look at food again in the same way. By the end of this course, students realize the profound connection between so many important things and food: food as sustenance, food as culture, food as ceremony, food as fun, and most essentially food as life."

*Bennett enjoying his healthy first birthday cake.*

# Lisabeth's Healthy Birthday Cake

*"This recipe balanced my desire to feed my little boy healthy food on his first birthday with the urge to see him elbow-deep in cake and frosting! I baked the cake in small star-shaped pans for his patriotic birthday and the recipe made about 16 stars. They freeze great, too."*

*-Lisabeth Abt Pieters*

(from <u>What to Expect the First Year</u>, Eisenberg, Murkoff, Hathaway)
Makes one double layer 9" square cake

## INGREDIENTS: for the Cake

2 1/2 cups thinly sliced carrots

2 1/2 cups apple juice concentrate (you'll use a little less)

1 1/2 cups raisins

Vegetable cooking spray

2 cups whole wheat flour

1/2 cup wheat germ

2 T. baking powder

1 T. ground cinnamon

1/4 cup vegetable oil

2 whole eggs

4 egg whites

1 T. vanilla extract

3/4 cup unsweetened applesauce

## DIRECTIONS

Combine the carrots with 1 cup plus 2 tablespoons of the juice concentrate in a medium-size saucepan. Bring to a boil, then lower heat, cover and simmer until carrots are tender, 15-20 minutes. Puree in a blender or food processor until smooth. Add the raisins and process until finely chopped. Let cool. (Hint: If you happen to have a commercial-strength blender, you can just put these ingredients in whole and blend.)

# First Birthday Cake cont'd

Preheat oven to 350. Spray pans with cooking spray.

Combine the flour, wheat germ, baking powder and cinnamon in a large mixing bowl. Add 1 1/4 cups juice concentrate, the oil, eggs, egg whites and vanilla. Beat just until well mixed. Fold in the carrot puree and applesauce. Pour batter into prepared cake pans.

Bake until a knife comes out clean, 35-40 minutes. Cool briefly in pans, then on wire racks to cool completely. Frost, if desired

# Pineapple Cream Cheese Icing

(from *Super Baby Food* by *Ruth Yaron*)

## DIRECTIONS

Mix in blender or processor:

1 – 8 oz. Package cream cheese

1/4 cup frozen pineapple juice

# Chicken Wing Wisdom IX

"*I have no idea how it happened. I randomly walked into the restaurant, not knowing anything more than my body was low on fuel. Two hours later, I walked out with a full stomach and an overflowing mind. Four women own and operate this restaurant. That fact by itself seemed like an interesting story to me. However, my editor thought otherwise and commanded I search further. So I returned--once, twice, three, ultimately four different times, and with each visit I managed to extract a greater essence of their shared story. Finally, I discovered that their remarkable Chicken Wing Wisdom and their partnered restaurant success all boil down to a simplistic motto they have hanging on their restaurant wall. It reads, 'Because nice matters'.*"

*"Because nice matters."*

*- unknown*

In 1991, researchers at Cornell and Michigan State Universities conducted a joint business study of restaurants in three independent markets. At the end of their ten-year investigation their research proved the following:

- After one year in business, 27% of the restaurants in the study failed.

- After three years in business, 50% were no longer serving.

- After five years in business, 60% had closed their doors.

- At the end of ten years, 70% of the restaurants that opened for business a decade earlier were "gone with the wind."

Apparently someone forgot to share these documented statistics with Sherry Biscaro, Annette Pulaff, Shelley Biscaro and Marina Ciesla, owners of Hamburg's The Poppyseed Restaurant. When the foursome purchased the popular South Towns eatery in 1999, not only were they facing overwhelming survival odds, their company books were sinking in $100,000 of red ink.

However, within a year of signing on the dotted line, these four determined women all but doubled the restaurant's gross income, wiped out their $100,000 debt, paid off the loan they originally secured to buy the restaurant, and gave raises and health benefit packages to their 17 employees. Five years after that, they joined the elite 40% of restaurants still in operation as they increased their catering and restaurant receipts by 400%, more than doubled the size of their staff, and significantly expanded their customer base to include regular diners from across Western New York, as well as Canada and Pennsylvania.

So how have these women accomplished this miraculous restaurant feat?  According to Annette, it's all according to a very simple plan.

"When we decided to buy the restaurant, we knew that with the large debt we would be in a tight spot.  But Sherry and I talked about it and we agreed that if we ran the restaurant as a way to help people and make a difference in their lives, rather than a way to make money, then it would be successful."

When questioned about the fiscal stability of their unusual business plan, Annette simply and directly offers.

"We didn't go into the business thinking that we could get rich. We went into it thinking we could give our employees raises and give them benefits, and that we could start making community donations---all the things that never happened at the restaurant until we took it over.  And when we sat down and talked with Shelley and Marina, we all agreed that it was what we wanted to do."

The selfless shared vision espoused by the quartet is not solely limited to employees' increased salaries and health insurance options.  According to Annette, the four owners have helped finance the first car for several of their young employees, occasionally forgiving the last few loan payments in lieu of a year-end bonus. They have also taken deserving employees on Caribbean vacations as a reward for jobs well done, and helped pay employee's personal bills in emergency situations.  They provide free uniforms for every staff member, offer catering services to employees at food-only costs, and regularly dole out seasonal and year end bonuses.  It's an unheard of management style, in a profession where 70% of all involved are virtually guaranteed to fail within ten years.

"Anytime we've ever made a profit, we've always given it back to our employees in the form of raises and loans," Annette states. "In fact, I've often joked that we should apply for not-for-profit status because while we are very profitable in our business, after we pay ourselves modest salaries, we take our profits and share them or give them away. Truly, we've never had an 'all about us' mentality and I think that's one reason we're so unique and we've become so successful."

The four women officially assumed ownership of The Poppyseed in September of 2000, each accumulating their individual restaurant expertise years before. Twin sisters Sherry and Shelley started out by working in their dad's West Seneca pizzeria at the age of seven. Annette, a neighbor of the Biscaro family, grew up working in a Greek restaurant with her father. Marina met Shelley at Ruby Tuesday's where they waitressed together for 12 years.

At the time the group took over The Poppyseed, all four had been working there for a number of years. Their long running relationships obviously serve as the key to their close and trusting work alliance. Still as in any business partnership, a competitive edge does exist within this group. It's a gentle strife centered on their corporate roles of Sherry as president, Shelley as vice president, Marina as treasurer and Annette as secretary.

"While we all have input, Sherry needs to be in control all the time," Annette bluntly proclaims. "It's either her way or no way."

Yet as quickly as the words are spoken, the close knit group offers praise for each woman's individual talents and abilities.

Their kind statements quickly soothe all ruffled feelings and Sherry to concludes their sibling-like rivalry with an executive declaration of peace.

"The dynamics of the 4 of us are so well balanced that we really complement each other extremely well. Even outside the restaurant we spend time together, we get together for the holidays. We're really like a family."

The concept of The Poppyseed as family is one that the owners regularly extend to their customers as well as their staff. Over and above the wealth of financial and personal support they provide for employees, these women make an effort to form true relationships with those who dine with them. They sit down and visit with customers as they enjoy their meals, they learn about their families, they celebrate their birthdays and they even help out those they know are in need. As for the food element in their customer service, chief cook Sherry offers The Poppyseed philosophy.

*The Poppyseed Restaurant owners (from left to right) Shelley, Sherry, Marina and Annette.*

"If someone comes in with a special dietary need, we are happy to accommodate them. If someone asks for something not on the menu that they just happen to want, if we can make it, we will. I've even had waitresses make a run to the nearby supermarket to accommodate a customer's special request. Those are the kind of things we are happy to do, and that people remember."

People also remember events that The Poppyseed caters. The owners initiated their off-site food service their first year in business. And despite the fact that the only promotional advertising they could afford was word of mouth, by the end of that first year catering proceeds paid off all of their corporate debt and supplied a healthy profit.

We've succeeded because we don't run our catering the way the textbooks say we should," Annette states. "When we meet with clients in their homes, we walk through the houses to get a feel of their personality. Then we individualize the menu to the people and the party. We're friendly and open and we serve beautiful food with unique garnishes and finishing touches that people enjoy and remember."

While Sherry, Shelley, Annette and Marina all place great importance on the quality of their food and the excellence of their customer service, there is a third element of their business that brings people, particularly women, back to The Poppyseed time and again.

"When women come in, especially in groups, they eat and hang out for hours and we encourage them to feel relaxed, as if there is no rush to get out," Shelley explains. "They really appreciate that and come back because of it. I also think they are happy when they find out that women own the restaurant and they want to support us."

The level of support that the four owners have earned from both their customers and staff was never more clearly evident than in the spring of 2005 when Sherry was involved in a motorcycle accident. As soon as word of the life-threatening crash reached Annette, she closed the restaurant for the first time in their five-year history.

"I knew no one would be able to concentrate on work while waiting to hear if Sherry was okay, so we shut down for the day. What I never imagined was that within hours, every member of our staff, all 37 of them, would show up at the hospital to wait for news. They sat outside and what I'll always remember is that every one of them were connected. They were holding hands or had their head on someone's shoulder. And no one left until they were able to go into Sherry's room and see for themselves that she was going to be okay."

While the hospital staff declared that Sherry was going to live, her injuries were many and severe. She broke six ribs on her left side, punctured her spleen, severely bruised and punctured her left lung and bruised her heart. Her ultimate prognosis was eight weeks of healing bed rest with mandatory in-home care. All of which meant that her 80-hour-a-week kitchen and food-ordering job was suddenly up for grabs.

Remarkably, within moments of receiving Sherry's long-term prognosis, the overwhelming task of how to run the restaurant without their beloved chef was solved. Shelley stepped forward to operate and coordinate the restaurant in concert with Marina. Staff members Laura, Jen, and Eric agreed to bridge any and all work gaps. Annette volunteered to act as Sherry's full time, live-in nurse. And The Poppyseed reopened on the day after Sherry's accident without any drop in service or sales.

To add to the story, in the weeks following her accident, flowers, phone calls and letters from caring customers overflowed Sherry's hospital room and her home. A significant trail of people also stopped by the restaurant to check on her progress. Most amazing was that five weeks after her motorcycle crash, Sherry walked through The Poppyseed's doors, into the office and began working part time.

As Sherry began to resume her full time restaurant responsibilities, her partner's personal and professional lives slowly returned to a level of normalcy. That is until another professional challenge rocked the close knit group. In July 2005, Annette took a leave of absence from The Poppyseed in order to open a restaurant in her hometown of South Dayton. She launched her culinary enterprise under the name of The Mustardseed in a building that originally served as her home.

*The Poppyseed Restaurant*

"I owned this big house and my daughter was getting ready to go to college and I really didn't need all the space," Annette states. "I wasn't sure what I wanted to do until one night some of the women from my church and I were sitting in my kitchen sharing food and conversation. We all started talking about how wonderful it would be to open a restaurant to benefit youth and church programs and also to create some jobs in our community. I started thinking about it and I realized that if I remodeled the upstairs of my house, I could create an apartment to live in and the downstairs could be turned into a restaurant. So that's what I did."

The Mustardseed's original staff was primarily composed of members from Annette's Free Methodist Church. While they were dedicated employees, they were, for the most part, inexperienced. Which is exactly why Annette took her leave of absence.

" I really wanted this restaurant to do well and so I made a commitment to spend a year cooking and training the people so that they could eventually run it themselves. I just felt that it was important for me to do it at that point in my life."

Annette's temporary departure initially caused hard feelings among her partners.

"We definitely felt deserted when Annette first told us she was leaving," Sherry states. "For five years we had a really good thing going and to lose 25% of our team made us wonder how it would effect our business. Annette is so amazing at what she does at the restaurant, there was no way to really know if her absence would be detrimental."

Fortunately, their bonds of friendship proved stronger than

their business ties, as Sherry states that by The Mustardseed's grand opening, all was well.

"When I was injured in the motorcycle accident, Annette gave her total support to me and to the restaurant by rearranging her life to move into my home and take care of me. Her actions were so kind and supportive that there was no way that we couldn't support her in return."

The most intriguing element of Annette's new restaurant venture is whether or not she will actually return to her Poppyseed roots? It is a question that she answers directly, with her trademark quiet strength.

"Absolutely. While I'm glad I've taken this time to devote to The Mustardseed, I look forward to getting back with Sherry and Shelley and Marina, and our wonderful staff and customers. It's like home to me and I love it there."

Each of these hard working women professes a true love for The Poppyseed, echoing Annette's sentiment of the restaurant as their home. When asked if any of them regret venturing into the highly demanding professional restaurant arena, the four respond as one, talking over each other in immediate praise of their shared experience. Then amidst laughter, Annette offers words that elicit nods of agreement from her partners.

"The experiences we have enjoyed here with our staff and our customers have brought so much to our lives. We've gotten to know the people who work and eat in this restaurant and to love them. We have one woman who tells us she comes in here because she feels like we're her family. And there are other customers who tell us that being in the restaurant feels like coming home."

And do these professional restaurateurs believe that in another five years they will again beat the odds by remaining as one of the 30% still in business? Without doubt or hesitation, they offer a group, "Yes," basing their shared conviction on a plaque hanging on their restaurant wall. It reads,"Because Nice Matters."

"In five years, I would hope that we will have grown together with our staff," Sherry states. "It's our dream to expand and open another restaurant that our employees can own and run, and hopefully we can increase both our salaries and our staff's salaries and continue to give back to the community. I know that the way we do business is not typical of other restaurants, but I like to think that we're blessed and succeed because of the way we do it."

While Annette offers the last word on the subject, again to group accord, "We'll succeed because of us. Because we are staff-centered, customer-centered, giving-centered and in every way, we share us. Our focus isn't the money. It really is in helping people and in making them happy while they're here, with us."

# Annette's Easy Meatballs

*"I included this recipe because my daughter and all of my family really like it. Hope you do too!"*

*-Annette Puleff*

## INGREDIENTS:

2 lbs. lean ground beef

1 lb. Sausage

1 cu. Bread crumbs

1 cu Parmesan/Asiago shredded cheese mix

1/3 cu finely diced onion.

1/2 cu minced garlic

1 t. pepper

salt to taste

## DIRECTIONS

• Mix all ingredients together.

• Form into meatballs.

• Add to sauce and simmer on low heat until cooked.

These meatballs taste better when made a day ahead.

If you are using sauce from a jar for your meatballs, you can dress it up with 1 large can of Italian Style tomato paste and 1 large can of Italian Style stewed or diced tomatoes. You can also add the parmesan/asiago cheese mix to the sauce for extra flavor.

# Marina's Chipotle Black Bean Dip

*"I love this dip. I can eat it for breakfast, lunch and dinner!"*

*-Marina Ciesla*

## INGREDIENTS:

2 lbs. blackbeans
2 roasted chipotle or jalapeno peppers
1 sweet roasted red pepper
1 t onion powder
1 t garlic powder
2 cu. Sour cream
Shredded cheddar and jack cheeses
Taco or corn chips

## DIRECTIONS

• Cook beans per directions on bag. Drain and let cool
• Toss together peeled and diced peppers.
• Blend together powders and sour cream.
• Fold beans and peppers into sour cream mixture.
• Top with cheeses.
• Serve hot or cold with chips.

# Shelley's Smoked Turkey Wrap with Cranberry/Apple Chutney

*"This recipe is semi-healthy and easy to make. I really love it."*

*-Shelley Biscaro*

## INGREDIENTS:

1/4 c. fresh cranberries or cran raisins

1 peeled and diced apple

1/4 c pineapple chunks

1 diced jalapeno pepper

1 t. fresh diced cilantro

1 T. cider vinegar

salt and pepper to taste

Herb flavored flour tortilla

Shredded romaine and iceburg lettuces

Diced walnuts

Shredded asiago cheese

Thinly sliced smoked deli style turkey

## DIRECTIONS

• Combine first seven ingredients to make chutney.

• Place all ingredients including chutney in center of tortilla.

• Roll tightly, cut and enjoy!

# Sherry's Fresh Basil Pesto Tossed with Chiffonade Vegetables and Penne Rigate

*"This is my favorite dish to eat anytime, anywhere, ever."*

*-Sherry Biscaro*

## INGREDIENTS:

1/8 c. toasted pine nuts

1/2 c. pecorino romano cheese

2 bunches fresh basil

1/2 c. extra virgin olive oil

Salt & pepper to taste

## DIRECTIONS

• Blend all ingredients in a food processor.

• Toss with your favorite pasta and chiffonade cut vegetables (carrots, red & yellow roasted peppers, portobella mushrooms, zucchini, red onion & eggplant) and serve.

# CHICKEN WING WISDOM X

*"I'd never met the woman whose house I was entering. In fact I'd never heard her name until close friends spoke of her as a Chicken Wing Wisdom Woman. As I sat down in her neat and tastefully decorated living room, I felt as if she was unsure of my presence -- as if she regretted agreeing to our interview. After jotting down several pages of my questions and her answers, I was still struggling to find the key that would reveal the wisdom of this woman's story. Then, one by one, her children began to wander in and out of the house, each one stopping to check in or be checked out. With each interaction, I witnessed the woman's caring character and her motherly love that obviously provided her true purpose. So I followed that lead and suddenly she was sharing stories about her extended family and her well-practiced cooking skills. She told me about her best recipes, filed away in her head, but stopped short of willingly sharing any single one. But she did explain that she learned her expert and widely enjoyed cooking talents by repeatedly making each dish over and over until she could make them all by feel, without even thinking."*

*"When you become a good cook, you become a good craftsman, first. You repeat and repeat and repeat until your hands know how to move without thinking about it."*

*-Jacques Pepin, French born chef, food columnist, cookbook author, and cooking teacher*

Nine children, two adopted children, 33 grandchildren, seven great grandchildren, over 60 foster children and a community full of people. Ask any of those listed above what they love about Bernice Redfern and they will all most likely give the same singular two-word response.

Her cooking.

At the age of 68, Bernice is revered by her family and renown in her community for the scrumptious meals she creates in her serviceable yellow kitchen set in the rear of her Butler Street home on Buffalo's East Side. It's a reputation that she proudly acknowledges has earned her the title by which she is known to young and old alike, "The Lady Who Cooks."

Bernice moved to Buffalo from Marshville, North Carolina in 1959 to care for her ailing sister. At the time, she was a married mother of two, firmly entrenched in the cooking traditions of her family's African American heritage.

"I was taught to cook pretty well by my stepmother," Bernice states. "She taught me how to make greens and beans, and cornbread. and grits, and biscuits, and I loved cooking them all."

As her family grew, Bernice's cooking excellence made her the "soul" provider for all of their catering needs. Virtually every family wedding, anniversary, graduation, and major

birthday party in the Redfern family has included a full buffet
of Bernice's down home culinary treats. From ribs and fried
chicken to greens and black eyed peas, macaroni and cheese,
potato salads and even, on occasion, chittlins, Bernice has been
the one and only chef of her family's choosing.

"My family tells
me that they love my
cooking and I really
don't know what's so
special about it, but
whenever they ask me
to make food, I don't
turn them down."

What long served
as her family's food
tradition eventually
transferred into a
practiced custom at
Bernice's Bethesda
Full Gospel Church.

*Dinner time at Bernice's (l to r) Barbara, Doris, Samantha, Germaine, and Gary.*

When fellow parishioners
got a taste of her fried chicken and her secret recipe barbecue, they
began singing her praises and requesting her talents. Soon Bernice
was serving as the chief cook at church fundraisers and picnics.
When word of her finger lickin' good food began spreading far and
wide, newspaper reporters vied to interview Bernice for the chance
to uncover her food magic recipes.

However, what everyone soon discovered about Bernice's
taste treats was that there were no recipes. In fact, a search of
her kitchen high and low easily proves that there is not one
cookbook or recipe card in this chief cook's domain. Instead

Bernice professes a reliance on her innate cooking sense and years of practice.

"A recipe doesn't mean anything if the food doesn't come out right," She states with a knowing attitude. "When I was a kid, I learned how to cook by doing. I would make something and if it didn't turn out I would have to do it again and again until I learned how. So I guess I learned to cook by feel. I cook things until they just feel right."

When asked if her unscientific food preparation method ever fails her, Bernice flashes an ear-to-ear grin and replies, "Only if I use a recipe."

While she may not rely on written instruction for her tempting meals, Bernice has created a sure-fire formula that has helped to maintain her family's well being and which she has passed through the generations.

"It's a rule in our house that everybody has to eat together at breakfast and dinner. I had to do it when I was young and I've carried it on with my own children and their children. It's a way to spend time together and I believe that it makes for closer relationships."

Bernice defines yet another element of her family's shared mealtimes that she believes provides long range value. "I think it's very important that children understand their heritage. So when I cook, I tell my children stories about the different dishes I've made. I tell them if it was one of their grandparents favorite foods or memories of something connected to the food. And they're always very interested and ask a lot of questions, which helps them to learn about who they are and where they came from."

*Bernice Redfern*

Throughout her life, Bernice has placed a high value on family traditions and ties. So she finds it disheartening to hear of children growing up in her community with no idea of their heritage. Yet rather than agonize over such circumstances, Bernice has found ways to change them. In 1966 she embraced the first of two children that she legally adopted. Over the subsequent 40 years she welcomed more than 60 foster children into her loving home. Bernice states, with a caring innocence, her reason for taking care of so many children.

"I was blessed with my own kids and I guess I just wanted to bless someone else's. Plus, as my kids got older I thought I would go nuts if I didn't have kids around the house. It's just too quiet and lonesome."

In assuming the responsibilities of foster care, one of the greatest challenges Bernice has faced is helping the children believe that they belong. Once again this wise woman has developed a recipe to deal with such difficulties that has turned out perfect everytime.

"The best medicine for these kids is talking and showing love. I sit down with them and ask them to tell me about their problems and the first thing they say is that no one loves them. I tell them that someone does love them---that I love them and God loves them--- and eventually I win them over."

This kind and caring foster mother also schedules regular family meetings as the "talking ingredient" in her successful child care recipe.

"It's always a certain night of the week, usually a Wednesday. We sit and talk and I ask them about their likes and dislikes, and how they feel about me. It's a good thing to do because it gives the children a chance to say how they feel, and it may be the very first time in their lives that they've been allowed to do that."

No matter what's happening in Bernice's warm and loving home, one thing is certain. It always smells like good food as soon as you walk through the door. Bernice notes that it's a tradition certified by family and neighbors alike. "If I barbecue, the whole neighborhood knows, because they can smell it around the block."

Bernice claims to be a fussy cook, insisting on specific ingredients in her meal preparation.

"I won't use canned or frozen foods when I cook. Only fresh. I like fresh."

Though as she begins to explain the cooking process for one of her favorite dishes, she suddenly hesitates in sharing her food wisdom. Finally she confesses the reason for her reluctance.

"I am protective of the way that I make my foods. I don't like to give away all my secrets because I wouldn't want anyone else to make food as good as mine!"

With formulas tucked away in her cook's know-how for tempting dishes like sweet potato pie, peach cobbler, beef rolls and salmon croquettes, one wonders what recipe Bernice favors most. After a brief pause for thought, she talks about an American classic.

*Bernice's son, Kenny, daughter-in-law Kim and granddaughter Kenetra enjoy one of her famous family barbeques.*

"A lot of people love my potato salad, but I love my macaroni and cheese. I use three kinds of cheese—longhorn, colby and velveeta--- and milk and butter. It's simple, but it's good." It's also the dish her son Ronnie requested upon his recent return from a tour of service in Iraq. Which again turns Bernice's attention to the subject of her children.

Family pictures overflow every mantle, window ledge and tabletop in Bernice's house. Her children along with her grandchildren and great grandchildren, obviously form the center of her world. In glancing through each room in her welcoming home, one finds a life study of family evolution and connection, with the woman in charge always faithfully in the background, stirring the pot.

"All of them come back. All of my kids come back with their families wanting to know what I've cooked and it makes me feel special that my cooking and the way I take care of my kids has made a difference in our family."

Looking forward, Bernice talks about her future birthday celebrations. Surprisingly, no one in her family cooks for Bernice on her special day. It seems that no one wants to prepare a meal and pale in comparison to the widely acknowledged cooking queen. Instead her children traditionally opt to take Bernice out to a restaurant. As for a birthday cake, Bernice professes a disregard for desserts, so there is no special sweet she desires. Gifts too fall in the category of unnecessary. Yet Bernice does keep in her heart a few birthday wishes that she hopes will one day come true.

"I wish that things for my family will continue to go well and that my children and grandchildren continue to stay healthy. And I wish that I get to see them all grow up and who they turn out to be. And I wish that they all learn to enjoy to cook for themselves and remember the things that I taught them about cooking. That's my wish. If my children carry on my cooking traditions, I would just love that."

# CHICKEN WING WISDOM XI

*"I really didn't want to write about this woman.
After all, what is there left to write about someone
who long ago plated up her own version of Chicken
Wing Wisdom in a story that has been told thousands
of times around the world? Yet, somehow it didn't
seem right to leave her out. So I made the pilgrimage
to the restaurant where she once cooked and served.
I studied the carefully preserved vintage photographs
on the restaurant walls that chronologically document
her life. I spoke with those who knew and loved her
best. Then I sat down at the computer and asked
for her guidance."*

*Do not follow where the path may lead.*
*Go instead where there is no path and leave a trail.*

*- Muriel Strode, author*

In considering Western New York Women who have used their innate sense of "food wisdom" to make a difference, it's impossible to ignore the woman who single handedly put Buffalo on the map by going where there was no path and leaving her own epicurean trail.

Teressa Bellissimo is the woman directly responsible for the creation of Buffalo Wings. As the now famous chicken wing story goes, Teressa was cooking in her Anchor Bar kitchen one Friday when her son, Dominic, came in with a late night snack request for himself and some friends. Short on available food, but long on creative cookery, Teressa took some meaty chicken wings she'd set aside for stock and threw them into the deep fryer. Once cooked, she smothered the wings in her secret hot sauce, partnered them with her home made blue cheese dressing, added a few celery sticks, and sent them on their way.

And that, quite simply, is how Buffalo's Chicken Wing tradition was born.

According to Teressa's niece, Rose Mary Bellissimo, her aunt's inventive cookery was nothing out of the ordinary.

"When my aunt cooked, she did her own thing. She didn't really follow recipes. If she wanted to make a certain dish with a certain flavor, she would just improvise and make it."

Yet outside the widely recognized details concerning the invention of Buffalo Wings, there are few facts known about the inventor herself.

Just who was Teressa Bellissmo?

*Teressa Bellissimo*

According to Ivano Toscani, long time employee and trusted friend of the Bellissimo Family and the current executive chef of the Anchor Bar, Teressa was an outspoken woman of Italian descent who devoted her adult life to the art of preparing food.

"Teressa stood about four-foot-eight inches tall and she was solid built, with dark hair and brown eyes," Ivano recalls. "She was very outgoing, but she had a feisty attitude and she didn't take any 'you-know-what' from anybody."

The only daughter of Sicilian immigrant parents, Teressa began her professional career by working for a telephone company. In 1934 at the age of 35, she gave up her office job to marry Frank Bellissimo. The following year, the two decided to partner in the running of an Italian restaurant.

The homestyle cooks began their culinary dream at an eatery that they established in partnership with Frank's brothers, Stephen and Carl. It was a small restaurant located in downtown Buffalo at the intersection of Canal Street and Dante Place alongside the Buffalo River. Their front window view of boats anchored nearby inspired the group to christen their establishment, Anchor Grill. Later, when Frank and Teressa assumed sole ownership of the family business and expanded it to its present

Main Street location, they reconfigured the name to the now internationally recognized, Anchor Bar. There for almost 50 years, Teressa and Frank lived upstairs, above the restaurant, and worked in the kitchen, downstairs. It was their life.

In the Anchor Bar's early days the husband/wife duo offered traditional Italian menu choices of pasta and sauce with meatballs or sausage, lasagna, bombers, and triple-decker sandwiches. What set the Bellissimo's menu offerings apart and contributed to their long-running success was that everything they served---from soup to dessert---was exclusively made by the two of them.

"Teressa was a great cook and she was very particular about everything," Ivano recalls. "It was Teressa's recipe for hot sauce and blue cheese dressing that helped to make the wings so popular. And we still use her recipes for many of the dishes that we prepare in the kitchen today. People love them."

Ivano adds that while the Bellissimos became well respected for their Italian cuisine, they were also celebrated for a Friday Night Anchor Bar Special completely unrelated to the preparation of food.

"On Friday nights there was always a band playing at the Anchor Bar and along about 11p.m., after the dinner rush was well over, Frank would bring Teressa out of the kitchen, still in her apron, and they would both join the band and sing. They had an act together that people loved.

During their late night performances Teressa would often warble Italian classics such as "Back to Sorrento," and "Oh How I Miss You," enchanting restaurant patrons as much with her voice as with her ethnic food specialties. Ivano recalls that Teressa was a unique vocal stylist.

"She would start singing the songs in English and often finish them in Italian. But no one cared. People just really loved her voice." To which niece Rose Mary adds, "Aunt Teressa had a beautiful voice and she always sang to perfection."

Although Teressa was a common sense woman when running the kitchen and creating the foods that made the Anchor Bar popular, Ivano notes she was also a woman ruled by a sense far from ordinary.

"Teressa would keep a piece of red cloth in her pocket at all times. She believed that the cloth kept 'Malocchio,' or the evil eye, away from her. She would also cut pieces from it and give it to people when they complained about having bad luck, to try and keep them safe. She was very superstitious that way."

*The Anchor Bar as it stood in 1951.*

As Ivano continues, it becomes apparent that Teressa's extra ordinary sense is still connected to the Anchor Bar today, 21 years after her passing.

"Teressa bought Frank a special diamond ring that he always wore and that she gave to me after he died. Since then I've lost it twice. Once in 1993, at Hamburg Beach, while playing with my dog. A lady picked it up out of the sand and brought it to me. I put it on my finger and when I looked up to thank her, she was gone, disappeared. Five years later, I lost it again and had no idea where. The night after I lost it one of the staff brought it to me. He found it in the grease pit in the kitchen. I know that Teressa had something to do with me getting the ring back both times. I know she and Frank are both here watching over the place too."

While Teressa became widely touted for her chicken wing legacy, all who knew her acknowledge that fame never mattered to the innovative cook.

"She really never was the kind of person to take credit for her accomplishments," Ivano states. "She was a very modest woman who just worked hard to make good food all of her life."

Despite her modesty, there is no question that Teressa's work ethic and tasty recipes helped to transform the Bellissimo's popular neighborhood bar and grill into an internationally recognized restaurant. From those early Buffalo Wing years when Teressa would plate up a hundred wings in an average day, the world has come to love and demand Anchor Bar chicken wings at the rate of 1,500 wings a day during the week and 7,000 daily on any given Saturday or Sunday. And that's not counting the thousands of wings special ordered and shipped to locations around the world. Ivano, who took care of Teressa in her later years after the passing of both her husband and son, believes that his one-time boss would be pleasantly surprised by this increased demand.

"Teressa had no idea that her wings were going to become so popular, but I think she would have been pleased that she created a sensation that helped to put Buffalo on the map."

In 1972, Teressa officially retired from her position of prominence in the Anchor Bar kitchen. Over the ensuing 12 years, she continued to live above the restaurant, coming downstairs each day to visit with patrons as they feasted on her traditional Italian dishes and ever popular chicken wings.

By the time she died in 1984, Teressa left behind a legacy of chicken wing wisdom that changed the lives of her family, impacted her community, and literally transformed restaurant menus around the world. All in all, quite an accomplishment for a woman who, according to her great nephew David Bellissimo, maintained a singular focus throughout her life.

"My great aunt was very jovial and very giving. She liked to sing and cook for people, make them happy. And while she was devoted to her husband and her son and her granddaughters Terry and Donna, it didn't matter if you were blood, she would take care of you no matter what."

David then offers an Italian translation that perfectly sums up this wise and wonderful woman.

"Our name, Bellissimo, means most beautiful. And that's just what Teressa was, a most beautiful lady."

# The Original Buffalo Wing Recipe Developed and Perfected at Frank & Teressa's Anchor Bar Buffalo, New York Birthplace of Buffalo Chicken Wings!

*INGREDIENTS:*

2 1/2 lb. fresh chicken wings (12-16 whole wings)

1/2 cup Original Anchor Bar Sauce

*DIRECTIONS*

• If preferred, split wings at joint, pat dry.

• Deep fry at 350 degrees for 10-12 minutes, OR

• Bake at 425 degrees for 45 minutes until completely cooked and crispy

• Drain wings.

• Put wings in bowl, add sauce and toss until wings are completely covered.

• Serve with bleu cheese and celery.

• For milder taste add additional margarine or butter.

# About the Author

*Photo by Roger Paris*

*Christina M. Abt*

Christina M. Abt is a nationally published essayist and magazine profiler. Locally her work has been published in a variety of newspapers and magazines including Buffalo Spree, The Sun Newspapers, Forever Young Magazine, Traffic East Magazine, EVE Magazine, The Buffalo News and online at Western New York Women.com. Christina is also a regular radio commentator for WBFO/NPR Radio where her "Heart and Soul" essays are broadcast on the first Wednesday of every month.

Christina's work has been featured in a number of Chicken Soup Books, including the most recently published *Chicken Soup to Inspire a Woman's Soul*. Additionally her essays have been published in the Heartwarmer's series of books as well as recorded on the Petwarmer's CD.

Along with her writing career, Christina works as part of the marketing/pr team for Lead Dog Communications, a virtual company headquartered in Charlotte, North Carolina, owned and operated by her son, James.

In between writing and public relations work, Christina breeds and raises World Champion Morgan Horses at her Crystal Hill Farm in Eden.

Christina is the wife of an awesome husband Michael; the mother of two terrific children Lisabeth and James; mother-in-law to a number one good guy, Kevin; Nana to one perfectly perfect grandson Bennett Christopher; And she will always be her mother's daughter.

# Birth of a Publishing Company

The Buffalo area's most innovative publishing company celebrated its 21st anniversary in 2005 by hitting a benchmark that few regional publishing houses achieve. Since 1984, Western New York Wares Inc. has moved more than 200,000 books and other regional products into homes, schools and libraries around the world.

Think of it this way. If we laid all the books we've distributed cover-to-cover in a paper path starting at the foot of Main Street near HSBC Center, the trail would stretch beyond the UB South Campus, snake through Williamsville, pass Batavia and end about 20 miles outside of downtown Rochester. Putting it a different way, we've distributed more than 25 million pages of information about our region. We could hand out individual pages to every man, woman and child in New York State and still have enough pages to supply half the population of Pennsylvania!

A pretty impressive path for a company that sprouted its roots in trivial turf.

The year was 1984 and the trivia craze was taking the nation by storm. As Buffalo journalist Brian Meyer played a popular trivia game with friends in his North Buffalo living room, he envisioned a game that tests players' knowledge about people and events in their hometown. Western New York Trivia Quotient sold out its first edition in six weeks and established Meyer as an up-and-coming young entrepreneur.

A year later, he compiled a book of quotations that chronicled the feisty reign of Mayor Jimmy Griffin. Meyer refuses to disclose how many six-packs were consumed while sifting through hundreds of "Griffinisms."

Meyer, a City Hall reporter for the Buffalo News, spent 15 years at WBEN Radio where he served as a managing editor. As

founder and president of Western New York Wares Inc., Meyer has collaborated with dozens of authors, artists and photographers. By 2005, the region's premier publisher of local books had been involved in publishing, marketing or distributing more than 125 regional products.

The Buffalo native is a graduate of the Marquette University, St. Joseph's Collegiate Institute and Buffalo Public School #56. He teaches communications courses at Buffalo State College and Medaille College. Meyer is treasurer of the Greater Buffalo Society of Professional Journalists' Scholarship Fund.

Meyer is assisted by Michele Ratzel, the company's business manager, and Tom Connolly, manager of marketing and distribution. The trio has a half-century of cumulative experience in regional publishing.

Ratzel is an administrative assistant at Daemen College. Connolly works as a news anchor and producer at WBEN Radio. He co-authored *Hometown Heroes: Western New Yorkers in Desert Storm*, a book published by Western New York Wares in 1991.

# About the Artist

Deborah Miller Gabler is a freelance artist who crafts and creates in her Shady Lane Designs Studio located in Hamburg, New York.

In her early career, Deborah worked as a professional stencil and wallpaper designer for a number of nationally known companies. Those particular design experiences led the talented painter to her current endeavor of creating artwork on the walls of homes and businesses throughout Western New York. Deborah's artistic talents, along with her intrinsic ability to create the exact image of her clients' dreams, have made her one of the area's most sought after decorative painters.

Deborah trained at the Art Institute of Pittsburgh. She also credits her great aunt for providing many of the learned techniques that have furthered her career.

Deborah is the proud mother of a grown daughter, Sarah. She lives with her tabby cat, Hobbs, in a charming cottage that is, of course, beautifully painted and decorated.

# Other Regional Books

Visit our Web site at **www.Buffalobooks.com** for a complete list of titles distributed by Western New York Wares Inc.

**Buffalo Soul Lifters: A Homespun Collection of Inspirational Stories** – What is it about Western New Yorkers that sets us apart from everyone else? Is it our iron will? Our unbending spirit? Our ability to see the glass as "half-full?" Author Frank Thomas Croisdale tells inspirational stories of local people who have achieved stunning accomplishments by believing in themselves and others.
*ISBN: 1-879201-48-8*                                                            *$12.95*

**Buffalo Memories: Gone But Not Forgotten** – The late George Kunz was blessed with a phenomenal memory. In his later years, he began chronicling his recollections of his Depression upbringing. For years, his anecdotes on everything from Bisons' games at Offermann Stadium to rides on the Canadiana and shopping excursions to 998 Broadway graced the pages of the Buffalo News. This book is a collection of about 200 of these anecdotes.
*ISBN: 0-9671480-9-X*                                                            *$15.00*

**The Mysteries of Father Baker** – This meticulously researched book documents why countless people throughout the world believe that Father Nelson Baker was a powerful miracle worker. Author John Koerner examines the historical record surrounding numerous wonders that have attributed to Baker's intercession.
*ISBN: 1-879201-49-6*                                                            *$12.95*

**Joe's Story: The Quietly Courageous Life and Violent Death of an Inner City Priest** – The riveting biography of the Rev. A. Joseph Bissonette, as recounted by his brother, Ray Bissonette.
*ISBN: 1-932-583-16-5*                                                           *$15.95*

**Hometown Tales: Beyond the Awning** – East Aurora businessman Ed Vidler serves up a collection of touching, amusing and insightful stories about life in small-town America. This delightful jaunt down memory lane includes pithy anecdotes from a man who works at the first and only job he has ever had – at Vidler's 5 & 10.
*ISBN: 0-9759700-1-1*                                                            *$9.95*

**Beautiful Buffalo: Preserving a City** – Buffalo has been called one of the most beautifully planned cities in the nation. America's great architects, including Frank Lloyd Wright, Louis Sullivan and Stanford White, helped make our city what it is today – a mecca for preservation pilgrims. Linda R. Levine and Maria Scrivani collaborated on a project that includes archival and contemporary photographs of many sites.
ISBN: 0-9740936-2-9                                                              $19.95

**Victorian Buffalo: Images From the Buffalo and Erie County Public Library** – Visit Buffalo as it looked in the 19th century through steel engravings, woodcuts, lithography and other forms of nonphotographic art. Author Cynthia VanNess has selected scenes that showcase everyday life and views of historic structures created by luminaries like Frank Lloyd Wright, Louis Sullivan and E.B. Green.
*ISBN: 1-879201-30-5*                                                            *$13.95*

**Frank Lloyd Wright's Darwin D. Martin House: Rescue of a Landmark** – The untold story of the abandonment and rescue of the region's most architecturally-significant home is recounted in vivid detail by Marjorie L. Quinlan. The book includes color photos and detailed architectural plans.
*ISBN: 1-879201-32-1*       *$13.95*

**National Landmarks of Western New York: Famous People and Historic Places** – Gracious mansions and thundering waterfalls. Battleships and nostalgic fireboats. Power plants and Indian long houses. Author Jan Sheridan researched nearly 30 National Historic Landmarks in the Buffalo-Niagara and Finger Lakes regions. Dozens of photographs, maps and an index.
*ISBN: 1-879201-36-4*       *$9.95*

**Classic Buffalo: A Heritage of Distinguished Architecture** – A stunning hardcover book pays tribute to the region's architectural heritage. Striking full-color photographs by Andy Olenick and an engaging text by Richard O. Reisem make this coffee-table book a keepsake for history buffs.
*ISBN: 0-9671480-06*       *$39.95*

**Church Tales of the Niagara Frontier: Legends, History & Architecture** – This first-of-a-kind book traces the rich history and folklore of the region through accounts of 60 area churches and places of worship. Written by the late Austin M. Fox and illustrated by Lawrence McIntyre.
*ISBN : 1-879201-13-5*       *$14.95*

**Symbol & Show: The Pan-American Exposition of 1901** – A riveting look at perhaps the greatest event in Buffalo's history. Written by the late Austin M. Fox and illustrated by Lawrence McIntyre, this book offers a lively assessment of the Exposition, bringing to light many half-forgotten facts.
*ISBN: 1-879201-33-X*       *$15.95*

**Western New York Weather Guide** – Readers won't want any "winteruptions" as they breeze through this lively book written by former Channel 7 weather guru Tom Jolls. Co-authored by Brian Meyer and Joseph VanMeer, the book focuses on historic and humorous weather events over the past century.
*ISBN: 1-879201-18-1*       *$7.95*

**White Death: Blizzard of '77** – This 356-page softcover book chronicles one of the region's most dramatic historical events. Written by Erno Rossi, the book includes more than 60 photographs.
*ISBN: 0-920926-03-7*       *$16.95*

**Great Lake Effects: Buffalo Beyond Winter and Wings** – a unique cookbook that is filled with intriguing historical facts about the region. The hardcover book has been compiled by the Junior League of Buffalo.
*ISBN: 1-879201-18-1*       *$18.95*

**Buffalo Treasures: A Downtown Walking Guide** – Readers are led on a fascinating tour of 25 major buildings. A user-friendly map and dozens of illustrations by Kenneth Sheridan supplement an enlightening text by Jan Sheridan.
*ISBN: 1-879201-15-1*       *$4.95*

**Buffalo's Brush With the Arts: From Huck Finn to Murphy Brown** – A fascinating adventure behind the manuscripts and million-dollar book deals, highlighting the Niagara Frontier's connection to many creative geniuses. Authored by Joe Marren, the book contains more than 20 photographs from the Courier-Express Collection.
*ISBN: 1-879201-24-0* $7.95

**Uncrowned Queens: African American Women Community Builders of Western New York.** Historians Peggy Brooks-Bertram and Dr. Barbara Seals Nevergold celebrate the accomplishments of African American women. Some of them are well-known; others have not received previous recognition.
*ISBN: 0-9722977-0-7* $11.95

**Buffalo's Waterfront : A Guidebook** – Edited by Tim Tielman, this user-friendly guide showcases more than 100 shoreline sites. It includes a handy fold-out map. Published by the Preservation Coalition of Erie County.
*ISBN: 1-879201-00-3* $5.95

**The Rainbow City: Celebrating Light, Color and Architecture at the Pan-American Exposition, Buffalo 1901** – The story of Buffalo's glorious moment, recounted in 160 pages and more than 20 images. Written by Kerry S. Grant of the University at Buffalo, the book chronicles an era when Buffalo was the nation's eighth largest city.
*ISBN: 0-9671480-5-7* $15.00

**Game Night in Buffalo: A Town, its Teams and its Sporting Memories** – Our region has enjoyed a storied sporting history. Sal Maiorana's books stirs emotions and passions as he recounts many never-to-be forgotten games and performances that fans have cheered and cursed. Many photos accompany a riveting text.
*ISBN 1-879201-44-5* $12.95

**Tale of the Tape: A History of the Buffalo Bills From the Inside** – Eddie "Abe" Abramoski reflects on scores on humorous, emotional and enlightening anecdotes that stretch back to the first Bills training camp in East Aurora. Many photos accompany the lively text.
*ISBN: 1-879201-41-0* $10.95

**Bodyslams in Buffalo: The Complete History of Pro Wrestling In Western New York** – Author Dan Murphy traces the region's rich wrestling history, from Ilio DiPaolo and Dick "The Destroyer" Beyer, to Adorable Adrian Adonis. Dozens of photos.
*ISBN: 1-879201-42-9* $9.95

**Haunted Places of Western New York** – Mason Winfield, the region's most high-profile paranormal investigator and 21st century "ghosthunter," pens a first-of-a-kind guidebook. Readers learn about "spooky communities" in the area, encountering haunted inns, highways, colleges and theaters. There are even chapters that focus on battlefield ghosts and grave haunts.
*ISBN: 1-879201-45-3* $12.95

**Spirits of the Great Hill: More Haunted Sites and Ancient Mysteries of Upstate New York** – From Mark Twain's Buffalo ghost, to Houdini's Halloween, Mason Winfield pens a riveting sequel to his supernatural survey of the region.
*ISBN: 1-879201-35-6* $13.95

**Shadows of the Western Door: Haunted Sites and Ancient Mysteries of Upstate New York** –
A supernatural safari across Western New York. Guided by the insights of modern research, author Mason Winfield pens a colorful, provocative and electrifying study of the paranormal.
*ISBN: 1-829201-22-4*        *$13.95*

**A Ghosthunter's Journal: Tales of the Supernatural and the Strange in Upstate New York** –
A delightfully diverse smorgasbord of strange encounters, all of them set in Western New York. The 13 fictional stories are inspired by the files of Mason Winfield.
*ISBN: 1-879201-29-1*        *$12.95*

**The Erie Canal: The Ditch That Opened a Nation** – Despite its shallow depths, the waters of the Erie carry an amazing history legacy. It was in canal towns like Lockport and Tonawanda where the doors to the American frontier were unlocked. Written by Daniel T. Murphy, the book includes dozens of photos.
*ISBN: 1-879201-34-8*        *$9.95*

**Seeing Niagara** – Discover 10 stunning vantage points that best showcase the majesty of the Mighty Niagara. Falls Historian Paul Gromosiak talked with 40,000 visitors, then weaved his findings into a book that's filled with fascinating facts, anecdotes and color photographs.
*ISBN: 1-879201-51-8*        *$8.95*

**Goat Island: Niagara's Scenic Retreat** – Historian Paul Gromosiak explores the people, attractions, animals and plants that makes the islands above Niagara Falls a fascinating destination. The book includes color photos and a detailed map.
*ISBN: 1-879201-43-7*        *$9.95*

**Nature's Niagara: A Walk on the Wild Side** – Learn more about the wild animals, plants and geological formations at Niagara Falls. Written by Paul Gromosiak, the book includes many full-color photographs and maps.
*ISBN: 1-879201-31-3*        *$8.95*

**Daring Niagara: 50 Death-Defying Stunts at the Falls** – Paul Gromosiak pens a heart-stopping adventure about those who barreled, boated, even bicycled to fame. The book includes vintage photos.
*ISBN: 1-879201-23-2*        *$6.95*

**Niagara Falls Q&A: Answers to the 100 Most Common Questions About Niagara Falls.** – Author Paul Gromosiak spent four summers chatting with 40,000 Falls tourists. This invaluable guide answers 100 commonly-asked questions. The book also includes photos, many of them in color.
*ISBN: 0-9620314-8-8*        *$4.50*

**Water Over the Falls: 101 of the Most Memorable Events at Niagara Falls** – Daredevils who defied the Mighty Niagara. Tragic rock slides and heroic rescues. More than 100 true-to-life tales are chronicled by local historian Paul Gromosiak. Color photos and vintage black-and-white photos.
*ISBN: 1-879201-16-X*        *$8.99*

**Zany Niagara: The Funny Things People Say About Niagara Falls** – A lighthearted tour of humorous happenings and historical oddities. Penned by Paul Gromosiak and illustrated by John Hardiman.
*ISBN: 1-879201-06-2*        *$4.95*

**Niagara Falls** – One of the world's most spectacular natural wonders springs to life in a book that contains more than 150 color photographs. From a visit in 1678 when a missionary recorded the first eyewitness account of the Falls, to an autumn day in 1993 when Dave Mundy became the only person to survive two barrel rides over the Niagara, readers experience an exhilarating tour. The book includes chapters on the Gorge, Niagara-on-the-Lake, wineries, the famous floral clock and Fort Erie.
ISBN: 2-84339-023-0                                                                                       $9.99

**The Magic of Niagara** – Viewing the Mighty Niagara for the first time stirs images of tranquility, power and magic. The story of Niagara is 12,000 years old, and author George Bailey skillfully captures the historical highlights in a book that contains a riveting text and more than 100 photographs. Sections include Niagara in the winter, the Maid of the Mist, famous daredevils and the Niagara Parks Butterfly Conservancy.
*ISBN: 0-9682635-0-X*                                                                                *$15.99*

**This is Niagara Falls** – Vibrant color photographs – more than 50 of them – capture the power and majesty of the Mighty Niagara. From the moment when darkness descends on this wonder and a dazzling display of lights appears, to the instant when the Maid of the Boat inches close to the foamy base of the Falls, this book captures the mystique of a this natural wonder.
*ISBN:  1-879201-38-0*                                                                                *$7.98*

**Toronto and Niagara Falls**– Two world-renowned destinations are showcased in one photo-packed book! More than 240 full-color photographs, a detailed street map, informative text and user-friendly index make this an invaluable companion.  Readers will explore Chinatown, museums, forts and gardens in Toronto. The Niagara Falls section highlights such attractions as Cave of the Winds and Maid of the Mist.
*ISBN:  88-8029-569-1*                                                                                *$15.99*

---

### Please include 8.25% sales tax for all orders in New York.

#### Also include shipping charges:

| Orders of | Please Add |
| --- | --- |
| Under $20 | $3.00 |
| $20 to $49 | $4.00 |
| $50 to $74 | $5.00 |
| $75 and Over | $6.00 |

*Visit our Web site at: www.buffalobooks.com or write for a catalog:*

**Western New York Wares Inc.**
P.O. Box 733
Ellicott Station
Buffalo, New York 14205

# Notes & Recipes